MADE IN HOLLYWOOD

All Access with the Go-Go's

GINA SCHOCK

BLACK DOG
& LEVENTHAL
PUBLISHERS
NEW YORK

Black Dog & Leventhal Publishers
Hachette Book Group
1290 Avenue of the Americas
New York, NY 10104
www.hachettebookgroup.com
www.blackdogandleventhal.com

First edition: October 2021

Black Dog & Leventhal Publishers is an imprint of Perseus Books, LLC, a subsidiary of Hachette Book Group, Inc. The Black Dog & Leventhal Publishers name and logo are trademarks of Hachette Book Group, Inc. The publisher is not responsible for websites (or their content) that are not owned by the publisher.

The Hachette Speakers Bureau provides a wide range of authors for speaking events. To find out more, go to www.HachetteSpeakersBureau.com or call (866) 376-6591.

Print book interior design by Douglas Brian Martin

Library of Congress Control Number: 2021930568

ISBNs: 978-0-7624-7497-4 (hardcover), 978-0-7624-7498-1 (ebook), 978-1-5491-3569-9 (audio download), 978-0-7624-7911-5 (signed edition)

Printed in Italy

ELCO

10 9 8 7 6 5 4 3 2 1

To my mother, June; my father, John; and my brother, Johnny,
I dedicate this book.

My grandparents Jean and Mitch, Anna and Duke.

The rest of my blood family and my extended family,
too many names to mention, but I believe you know who you are.

Penny, my little angel and constant companion.

Moe, Dottie, Walter, Ike, Ethel, Noodles, Floyd, and Fritz,
never forgotten.

Contents

Behind the band, most of the time, sits the drummer. She sits on a stool, adjustable and padded, commonly referred to as "the throne." Maybe that's because, really, the drummer rules the band. The drummer is the one who determines the tempo of the songs. Sometimes she may have to imperceptibly pull back when it's going a little too fast or push the players to speed up if it's dragging. You best follow along—do as your drummer dictates—or else it's on you, for making things sound like a mess. The drummer is the one responsible for the dynamics of the song, the one who makes sure the intensity builds or that the sound is pulled back, so that the audience can focus clearly on the vocals. The drummer cues the long, drawn-out endings that stop on a beat after a wild, peaking roar of instruments. The drummer commands the energy: her fills, rolls, and power infuse the song. The drummer, if it's Gina Schock, also gives the songs identifiable hooks—instantly recognizable, the heartbeat and life-force of a track.

Besides ruling the band, only the drummer gets to have the view from the throne. It must be something to see—the whole band is in sight, their glorious backsides imperishably imprinted upon her mind. A glance to either side and she will see how the crew is doing, attentive and ready to take care of any problems. She can see the monitor mixer clearly, as well as the sound board up ahead in the midst of the audience. And she sees the entirety of the crowd—the ones smashed at the front of the stage, close enough to make eye contact, all the way back to the fans dancing in the bleachers. She takes in the long-range scenery of the venue and can find in an instant the close-ups of all her bandmates' facial expressions. Nobody

The View from the Throne

except the drummer gets this panoramic, zooming in, zooming out view from the throne. I'm telling you all this to underscore a truth at the core of this book: It is no surprise and it's no accident that Gina has a perspective unlike anyone else in the band.

I could tell you stories, lots of stories, from my point of view. Any of the Go-Go's can do that. But only Gina can tell you her stories and *show you*, actually show you, what she was seeing. Her perspective manifested in photographs from the very beginning, when she joined the Go-Go's. Gina whipped the potential of the band into straight-up contenders for everything that followed and documented the whole ride. It's one thing to casually take pictures; it's another thing altogether when the photographer is one of you. We trusted her and let her rule and direct us, just like she did from the throne behind the drums. The Go-Go's, always ready to laugh with one another or at one another, were happy to act out Gina's vision or scenario for what would make artful Polaroids or a well-composed shot. She kept her favorites and brought them on the road, and time and time again she pulled them out so we could all gather around and collapse in gales of laughter at the moments she had captured.

There is a determination and pureness to Gina's focus. I've seen it, not only in her musicianship and songwriting but also in her life and in her judgment as to what is important to her. All the elements that make her a great drummer are evident when you know her: a methodical and precise organization for the external details that make up her day-to-day—and the explosive and deep emotion she bestows on her loved ones. Deciding to create this book was a task she undertook with the same passion and work ethic she has called on throughout her career. It has been compiled, from inspiration to completion, with the same thoughtfulness and tangible effort she devotes to friendships and favorite causes. And while the pages might tell the stories of her band, from the anecdotes of the friends she has made along the way to her own recollections, it's the photos, from behind the scenes, that tell the most evocative accounts.

Gina sets her seat low and her cymbals high— every crash is a reach for the sky. I used to think it was for sight lines, so everyone could get a clear view of her as she propelled the Go-Go's through countless delirious concerts. One day at sound check I went and sat behind her kit and realized this setup enhanced her vision. The configuration is as purposeful and thought-out as any construct she undertakes; it gives her exactly what she needs to keep the energy flowing between the kit, the band, and the fans. On behalf of Gina, I invite you to go forward in these pages, knowing that you are now part of the gang, gathering around to enjoy the surprises and stories that the pictures tell.

Kathy Valentine
Austin, Texas

Baptism by fire. That's what I'd call my first concert—Led Zeppelin opening for the Who in 1969 at Merriweather Post Pavilion in Columbia, Maryland. My brother was recruited to take me because I was only eleven years old at the time. Seeing and hearing Zeppelin live was like experiencing a controlled explosion. It blew my mind! Robert Plant had the voice of an angel and the moves of a sinner. Jimmy Page had command of his guitar like nobody else. John Paul Jones was solid and seemed like the glue holding it all together. The drummer John Bonham was steady and powerful, moving around the kit with lightning speed and leading the band as much as anyone else. Then came the Who. Those guys really

knocked me out. They had it all down. Roger Daltrey was so handsome with incredible stage presence. Pete Townshend was a dynamo. I watched as his guitar became an extension of himself. The bass player John Entwistle had a very busy style. His fingers seemed to be all over the fret board at once. Don't get me started about Keith Moon. No one has ever played like Keith Moon, a style that cannot be replaced. At the end of the Who's performance they destroyed their instruments. I was absolutely enthralled. What a finale. After seeing these two performances, all I could think about and dream about was being on that stage. What position I was in didn't matter. It seemed I had figured out what I wanted to do with the rest of my life. Music, so big, so wide, so reaching and it had me in its grips just where I wanted to be.

The next concert was Black Sabbath at the Baltimore Civic Center, which was located downtown. I would take a bus there, and then my mom picked me up afterwards. That show left a powerful impression on me as well. Black Sabbath was one of my favorite bands. I needed to start documenting what I was seeing. Not having a lot of money, I went out and bought a little Instamatic. Eventually, I got a 35-millimeter camera that I took with me to every show. Rod Stewart; J. Geils Band; Alice Cooper; Hall & Oates; Grand Funk Railroad; Sly and the

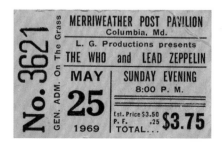

No. 3621 GEN. ADM. On The Grass

MERRIWEATHER POST PAVILION
Columbia, Md.

L. G. Productions presents
THE WHO and LEAD ZEPPELIN

MAY 25 1969 | SUNDAY EVENING
8:00 P. M.

Est. Price $3.50
P. F.   .25
TOTAL... $3.75

Let the Show Begin

Family Stone; Humble Pie; Yes; ZZ Top; New York Dolls; David Bowie; Deep Purple; Emerson, Lake & Palmer; Steve Miller Band. The list goes on and on. All that I was experiencing filled me up. The music was speaking to my soul, and finally the images in front of the lens were being recorded.

During my initial drive from Baltimore to Los Angeles in the winter of '79, I had a camera around my neck taking photos. From the beautiful vistas surrounding me on Interstate 10 to the eventual room the Go-Go's first rehearsed in (stinky, smelly, and below a porn theater), I was putting something together and unknowingly becoming the archivist of the band. Whenever the moment struck me, I started clicking away. Perhaps the band backstage after a show having a lot of drinks with our colorful friends, or touring the entire country in agony stuck in a twelve-seater van, or even playing the Rock in Rio festival in front of 250,000 people, there's been much to take in and take from. All that we've experienced has become a testament to our passion and tenacity.

In the early days playing clubs, I would always look for a poster or a flier from the show we were about to do. As we started touring, it was backstage passes, Go-Go's T-shirts, tour books, and more. One of my favorite types of photography became Polaroids. During the process of putting together *The Go-Go's* documentary, I again was inspired to rediscover all that I was saving. There was so much I wanted to show that had been sitting in drawers, stuffed in closets, and shoved under the bed over the past forty years. I know you folks have heard this cliché a million times, but this book truly is a labor of love. The band has been encouraging me for several decades to put it together. The Go-Go's have always been about positivity, acceptance, and really just simply wanting to make people feel good whether they come to a show or listen to one of our songs. Looking through all that I have saved, I am thankful I kept so much. Music and fashion are cyclical. If you hold on to stuff long enough, it comes back into vogue. This book is the summation of that. I entitled it *Made In Hollywood* because that's where it happened. I met the Go-Go's there, became a Go-Go there, and that will never change.

We hadn't released a new song in almost twenty years, and then we put out "Club Zero." It landed in the top 10 of *Billboard*'s Rock Digital Song Sales chart. That is directly due to our fans. I think we represent a lot more than we ever imagined we would. Being part of the women's movement is certainly one of our accomplishments. When I am reminded of our contributions, I'm in disbelief. It continues to humble me to this day. So many important moments in my life are revealed throughout the pages of this book. I have done it as a big thank-you to the fans. They were in the clubs, they were there in the arenas, and even during the period of time when the band broke up, the fans never left. They encouraged us to get back together and make music. *God Bless the Go-Go's*. God bless the fans.

Now . . . have a look through my eyes.

Gina
San Francisco, California

We All Need
Good Teachers

The first time I picked up a bass guitar, I really thought that since it had only four strings, how difficult could it be to play? It was Japanese, a Dia, looking pretty cool and professional just like a Fender P Bass. The issue was that the neck of the bass was thick and my little hands could barely fit around it. I bought it at old man Petro's music store up on Eastern Avenue in the Highlandtown neighborhood of Baltimore. His shop was not far from my house. I'd ride my bicycle there and look around and see what I could afford. Every penny of my allowance was put into what I will now call my music education. The more I learned, the more I wanted to know. By the way, the bass is not an easy instrument to play. Don't let the four strings fool you!

Mom and Dad were great teachers. Music seemed to be a part of all of our lives. It was sometimes in the forefront, sometimes in the background, but always there. While my brother, Johnny, was playing *Beggars Banquet* by the Stones, my parents were singing and dancing to song after song by Count Basie. We heard his records the most in our household. I had my ear glued to a transistor radio that I carried with me at all times. I was usually listening to 101.5 WBAL and would call the station to request my favorite songs, most of the time waiting hours for them to be played. Around five o'clock every day was dinnertime. Dad would put a record on for us to listen to while we ate. When I think back, my parents were pretty edgy when we were kids. They liked to go out, see a band, dance, and have a good time. The first boyfriend my mother ever had was my father. June and John were high school sweethearts. I know that sounds hokey, but they really were. (Things like that do happen.) When they got out of high school, they married, and the next seventy-two years of their lives were spent together very much in love. Growing up in our house was a beautiful place to be.

For me, the best part of the day was when I had an hour or so to practice. I messed around with the bass for several months and then moved on to guitar, but I soon realized that it wasn't going to work either. Then came the drums. You have your kick pedal, cymbals, stands, sticks, and then of course all your drums. There are a lot of pieces that put a kit together, and that takes money. It would be several months of accumulating my allowance for the picture to be complete. Finally, I set up the kit in my bedroom, which was perfect, because my stereo was there. When I sat down and started to play, it was easy; I didn't have to think. I knew I had found my instrument.

There are songs that you just want to listen to, and then there are songs that you want to play. Cat Stevens was definitely in the "listen to" category with his soft, melodic voice. Just think of "Morning Has Broken" or "Wild World." They are entrancing. I was so in love with him that I cut out his head shot from *Teaser and the Firecat* and taped it right next to my bed. Looking at that beautiful face made me feel dreamy. Now, if I was thinking of a band that made me want to get up and groove, that would be Aerosmith. "Sweet Emotion" was always a blast to play. The choices that drummer Joey Kramer made were the right ones for the song. His playing is creative, dynamic, and precise. He is an exceptional drummer and I feel a bit underrated. I would put my headphones on and play to my favorite records as if nothing else mattered. This would go on for hours until, eventually, I developed blisters. I didn't care that my hands were throbbing, because the music just swept me away.

My thinking was very much counterculture punk. I had a lot of pent-up anger. I am not sure what it was about or where it came from, but it was inside me. The trick was to funnel it all into my love of music. When it came time to join a band, I wanted like-minded musicians. I found Scratch 'n Sniff. They were looking for a drummer, and I was constantly looking to join a band that I could call my own. Guitarist George Kondylas, bassist

Charles Freeman, and lead singer Danny Brown were the three musicians who made up Scratch 'n Sniff. I had to audition, so George and Charles came over to my house. I sat down, put my headphones on, and started playing. I really wasn't that nervous because all of us were from the same neighborhood. I was comfortable, closed my eyes, and focused on what I was playing. That was the way I relaxed into a song. George later told me that within the first thirty seconds he turned to Charles and said, "This is going to work. We found our drummer."

I was excited to be playing with musicians the likes of George and Charles. They were miles ahead of me. I knew I would learn a lot from these guys . . . and I did. Our music choices were very eclectic. We were doing songs by Brian Eno, Lou Reed, the Vibrators, and the Ramones, just to name a few. And as his ultimate fan, I always looked forward to playing the eight-minute Bowie medley. Summers in Baltimore are so humid that when you try to breathe it feels like there is no oxygen in the air. When we were rehearsing, we kept the windows open in Charles's basement. One night, in the middle of a song, a young police officer showed up. A neighbor had complained that the music was too loud. The cop was a nice guy and definitely interested in what we were doing. He asked us to keep on playing and did we mind if he stayed for a while to have a listen? We kept on playing, and twenty minutes later, we had a new friend and fan.

The four of us got along really well, and so the music came together quickly. We got a manager, Christine Mason, who was mostly known around town for doing all the hairdos in John Waters's films. Chris started to get bookings for the band. She was a good manager and a tough cookie, respected by those she dealt with. One of the gigs she booked for us was at the Marble Bar. It was in the downstairs of a hotel, with a really long marble bar that was both impressive and inviting. Many of the bands that came through town played there, including Blondie and Talking Heads. It was the hippest, coolest place to play in Baltimore. This was a big deal for us. We played four forty-five-minute sets. The majority of the songs were covers. We also did a set of originals. "Rawhide" and "Diamond Rio" were two of my favorites. Although we rehearsed a lot, playing live was a different animal. A microphone going out in the middle of a song or a bad connection between an amp and a guitar—things could go wrong, and occasionally they did. But George liked to say,

LIVE ON STAGE ▶

ALL GIRL PUNK ROCK BAND

ACCLAIMED STAR OF "PINK FLAMINGOS"

MISS EDIE and the INCREDIBLE EDIBLE EGGS

Miss Edith Massey;"Miss Edie the Egg Lady", fronting her own all girl PUNK rock Band

Advance Tickets $5 on Sale at Theatre

3 Shows   **7 pm**   **10 pm**   **1 am**

NUART NOV. 4

11272 SANTA MONICA BLVD. WEST L.A.   478-6379 & 479-5269

"What you lack in proficiency, you make up in energy." That certainly applied to Scratch 'n Sniff.

I moved out of my parents' house at nineteen and got a studio apartment in Fells Point. Edith Massey, the star of many John Waters films, had her thrift store there, Edith's Shopping Bag. She was a self-described "B-girl." I would walk down to her shop several times a week just to sit and talk with her. She was such a sweet old lady, and I grew to really care about her. One day when I went to visit her, she said in that incredibly distinct Edie voice, "Gina, I want to put together a punk band. Do you want to be in it? We're going to go to Philadelphia, New York, LA, and San Francisco." I couldn't get the words out fast enough: "Yes, of course, Edie!" This was opening the door to a path of opportunity I had been hoping for. Obviously, there weren't any record labels in my hometown, and I knew that I'd have to go to New York, San Francisco, or LA if I had any chance of making it. The music scene in those three cities was incredibly vibrant during that period of time, especially the punk scene.

Edie and the Eggs were born, the shows were booked, and our mini tour began. The drive to New York City was a good one, as I had taken that trip so many times with my parents. I was thrilled to be playing at Max's Kansas City. Max's was an upscale punk bar that everyone in the new music scene knew about. The New York Dolls, Iggy and the Stooges, and the Patti Smith Group were just some of the bands that played and hung out there. It was quite an accomplishment to be doing one of my first shows at Max's. Along with CBGB, they were *the* two premier punk clubs on the East Coast that you wanted to play at.

I was twenty-one, and I'd never been on a plane before, so my flight to LA was a first. I remember boarding the plane being fearful and exhilarated at the same time. The trip seemed to take forever. I could feel the anticipation growing the closer I got. As I looked out the window, it turned from flat land to the majestic Rocky Mountains to Los Angeles. When we were descending, the city seemed to stretch as far as the eye could see—a massive expanse of humanity. We were picked up at the airport by one of the Martin brothers. Doug Martin was a tall, lanky, well-spoken, gentlemanly kind of guy with a shock of red hair on his head. He greeted us with a much-welcomed big smile and an invitation to see the city. Edie was booked at a Holiday Inn off the 405. The whole trip was low budget, so myself and the other bandmates stayed at Doug's brother's house. Steve Martin (the filmmaker not the comedian) lived in a two-bedroom shack nestled in between multimillion-dollar homes off of Beverly Glen. When we pulled up and Steve came out, my jaw dropped. I was looking at identical redheaded twins. Steve and Doug spoke the same, dressed the same, and had the same mannerisms. You really had to know them to be able to tell them apart.

Edie and the Eggs were scheduled for three shows at the Nuart, a hip art house movie theater. It was charmingly run-down, and Steve was the head projectionist there. Cult films were played every weekend, which always drew an interesting crowd. For our performance, Steve had to order a stage and a PA system. Then they pulled out all the stops and had a backdrop made—a large piece of clear plastic with "Edie and the Eggs" spray-painted on it. High art, right? In the middle of sound check, a colorfully dressed little pixie of a girl with a camera skipped down the aisle and started shooting photos of Edie and the band. Her name was Relah. She was funny and quite eccentric. I knew she and I would become good friends.

It was 1978, and any crowd that followed John Waters's films would most likely be a wild bunch. This was prior to the huge commercial successes that awaited him. One of the biggest stars of his filth academy was about to hit the stage. The audience was already getting rowdy. Edie stood hidden behind the amps while the band played several songs, working the crowd into a frenzy. When she made her entrance, the whole place went berserk. She came out swinging a big plastic sword and wearing her signature black leather catsuit from *Female Trouble*. What a woman! The songs were a bunch of chords and words thrown together in a hasty fashion. Not a lot of thought and very little time was spent crafting them. Nevertheless, I think everyone was thoroughly entertained. Did I mention we had to do three shows that evening? Seven p.m., ten p.m., and one a.m. In between shows, we were taken to a party at Fiorucci in Beverly Hills. I believe it was an art opening, or that's the way it looked to me. Steve, Doug, and Relah escorted us in. The place was packed with press, paparazzi, lots of mohawks, and crazy-colored hair. A huge room, and in every direction you looked something was going on. This was my first real Beverly Hills party.

Phily | Grendel's Lair
500 South
#215 - 9...

($1/00 Clean)

N.Y.C. | CBGB's   Sept. 27, 28 + 29
Bowery   Wed., thru., Fri.

$1,000.00 + 50% of door   35 minute
guaranteed   sets

Hilly Crystal (owner) (212)-254-4517
Charles Martin (stage man) 982-4052   180.
Linus + Norman stage crew   clear

Phily | Artimus Club   Oct. 9th
2300 Walnut St.   (Sat.)   2 sets
Suite 521, Phily, Pa.   35 minutes

$300.00 plus 60% of door   Rip-off!

David Carroll (manager)

N.Y.C. | MAX'S   Oct. 18 & 19   (150
213 Park Ave. (South)   Wed., thru.   clear
212-260-0343
                    Terry Ork, (manager)
                    Peter (manager)

$175.00 plus 70% of door.

San Francisco was our next show. We were booked at the Warfield Theatre, which was a proper venue where bands played regularly. This was probably the most professional setting of our mini tour. After that show, we were taken to several clubs and then to Mabuhay Gardens, a place I had heard and read about. It was San Francisco's most fashionable punk club at the time, and I was very excited to be there. What a way to end the tour. I flew back to Baltimore knowing it wouldn't be long before I would be leaving for good. One of the first things I did when I got home was have a conversation with my parents. They were my rock. I dreaded letting them know the decision I had come to. The funny thing is I wasn't the least bit worried about walking away from my comfort zone in Baltimore and making this crazy journey. My mind was made up. I was leaving.

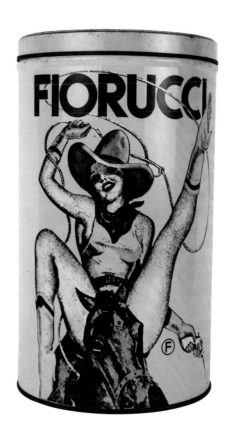

Perfect Place, Perfect Time

The day had finally come and I was about to embark on the three-thousand-mile journey that would take me to my new home somewhere on the West Coast. I didn't know where I would end up. I had let go of my apartment and moved home a couple months before I was planning on leaving. My mother and father were waiting at the bottom of the steps. This was the moment I dreaded, saying goodbye to the two people who loved me unconditionally and who I loved more than anything else in the world. The thought of being on the other side of the country made my heart ache, but I assured them that I would drive safely and check in at the end of every day. Finally, I burst into tears when Mom and Dad were hugging me. My mother said over and over, "If it doesn't work out, you know you can always come home." These are important words to hear when you're leaving. They stayed in my head the entire drive, and to this day they have never left me: "You can always come home." I felt like Dorothy in *The Wizard of Oz*.

I walked to my dad's pickup to give it one last final check before I hopped in. He had constructed a wooden cab to cover the bed of the truck. The drums, PA system, stereo with huge speakers, clothes, guitar, bass, amps, all my vinyl, and then some were stuffed in the back. And my high school friend, Babs, was making the trip with me. It was so nice to have someone to talk to over the many hours we would spend together driving. When I left Baltimore, there was no way I was coming back a failure. My parting words to everyone were, "The next time you see me, I'm gonna be a rock star."

Valentine's Day of 1979, we drove into a Chevron station in West Los Angeles. I turned the ignition off, jumped out of the truck, and headed to a pay phone in the parking lot. The first call I made was to my friend Steve, who had produced the Edie and the Eggs show at the Nuart. We had kept in contact over the last several months. His faith in my ability to succeed gave me even greater confidence to make the trek to LA. Steve was terribly kind to let me stay at his house until I was able to find a place of my own. The house had a great view of the canyon from the back porch, and that was mostly where everyone hung out. However, the whole structure seemed really flimsy. Every party that we had—and there was one just about every weekend—I was convinced the house was going to slide down the hill. We had some crazy times at that funky old joint.

I was putting my name and information in all the music stores on and around Sunset Boulevard. The drums and PA system were set up in Steve's living room so I could sit down at the kit and play whenever I felt like it. Needing to get a job, I wound up at Odie's Market up the street on Beverly Glen. It was a real neighborhood store, a leftover from the sixties. Working there was always interesting. One afternoon while eating my lunch, sitting in front of the store, a Mercedes pulled in. On the passenger seat sat George Harrison. I couldn't believe one of the Beatles was ten feet away from me. His wife Olivia got out of the car to grab something from the market. Later I found out we were neighbors. They lived a little farther up the hill. Beverly Glen was filled with artists, actors, musicians, and writers. It was a very artsy community, and I loved being a part of it.

The phone started ringing. There were lots of calls from bands that were interested in me. Of course, they were all guys, but I was used to that. I guess they loved the novelty of having a female drummer. I ended up joining a band with a group of guys who were good musicians. What a relief to finally be able to play with someone. I missed hanging out with other musicians and talking music. Unfortunately, the more we rehearsed, the more I realized this wasn't going to work. But I continued to play with them and in the meantime kept going to shows and meeting new people, hoping to find the right fit.

The punk scene in LA was happening in a major way. One of the many things I loved about this scene was its inclusivity. Come to the shows. Be who you are. Say what you want to say. Being a punk didn't necessarily mean you had to look any particular way.

You didn't have to dress like the Sex Pistols with a safety pin in your ear or your nose. Everybody had their own look, and we were all edgy. I was edgy in my own way but in true need of a makeover. That makeover would be coming quicker than I knew. Steve took me to all the clubs, and we saw lots of different bands. There was one in particular that he wanted me to see right away. The band was the Go-Go's. And though they hadn't been around that long, they already had a bit of a following. Two days later, Steve and I were at Club 88, watching them play. I immediately fell in love. Dressed in loud Day-Glo colors, wearing severe makeup, and acting tough with their cherubic little faces, they were having so much fun onstage screaming out, "Come join us" without actually saying the words. So inviting. You wanted to be a part of this.

Seeing the Go-Go's perform had changed my mind-set. I realized you could have a lot of fun playing. It didn't have to be so serious. Steve's brother Doug called me to let me know that he was having a party at his house in Santa Monica. Both brothers were well connected in the film and music scene, and I knew this would be a fun get-together. Not that I can remember a lot from that evening, but I do remember that the music was loud, and everyone was friendly, high, and having a good time. Someone introduced me to Jane and Margot from the Go-Go's. Jane had a very bubbly personality, and Margot reminded me of some people that I grew up with back east. She seemed like trouble, and I liked that. One of the first things they said to me was that they were looking for a drummer. So I said, "I'm a drummer, and I'm looking to join a band." We hung out for quite a while and talked about music, the punk scene, and what it all meant to us. It was then decided they would come over to Steve's house, and we would play some songs and see how it went.

Belinda, Charlotte, Jane, and Margot walked into the living room with their instruments in hand. They acted pretty nonchalant about being there, but you could tell there was a serious tone to our meeting that day. They definitely wanted a new drummer. Charlotte pulled out a cassette that had several Go-Go's songs on it from a rehearsal. They played it . . . I listened. The one that really stuck out was "Beatnik Beach." It was a real drummer's song, and I loved playing it. I came up with my own version using different tom-toms and changing up the beat slightly. I knew it was good, and I think they knew it too. We all started smiling, and that was the way it was for the entire rest of the evening. There was a palpable connection. We liked the same things, the same kind of music, and we loved Bowie. I also had a truck that we could haul the gear around in. That didn't hurt. I knew that I would quit the other two bands the next day and they would fire their drummer.

The next week I wound up moving all my gear to their rehearsal space at the Masque. The Masque was located in the basement of a porn theater called the Pussycat. It was stinky, filthy, and the perfect place for us to party and play whenever we felt like. There was always something happening at the Masque. We shared our rehearsal space with several other bands. When we started going over songs, it was obvious that the majority of them needed some work. We began the process. I tried to ingrain in the girls that we had to spend more time practicing if we were going make something of this band. I believed the Go-Go's could be successful, they just needed to be pushed a lot harder. The main thing we needed to concentrate on was the arrangement of material we already had, but writing new songs was just as important. Thankfully, everyone got on board with this idea.

A show had been booked at Hong Kong Cafe for July 20. That meant I had a little over a month to learn all the songs and hopefully be able to back them up by playing with a little confidence. We always had fun at rehearsals, but now we had to get down to work. The thing that stands out the most in my memory about the show is that it was supposed to be a fifty-minute set and I wound up doing it in half an hour. My confidence went right out the window. I was incredibly nervous and played the songs so fast it was hard for Belinda to get the words out of her mouth. But at the end of the day that really didn't matter because it was about being somewhere super cool on a Friday night, hanging out with our friends, and becoming part of a scene. Everyone was having a great time, and so were we, completely engaging with our audience. The songs were played with speed and conviction. We were a punk band and proud of it.

Like many good things in life, my involvement with the Go-Go's started by accident. What seems like a million years ago, but at the same time like yesterday, I was working at the hippest art movie theater in Los Angeles, the Nuart. For a film student, it was paradise. Every Friday at midnight we showed David Lynch's *Eraserhead*, and every Saturday at midnight, Baltimore's Prince of Puke, John Waters's *Pink Flamingos*. So it was only natural that when Edith Massey, the Egg Lady in *Pink Flamingos*, formed a punk band, the Nuart was the perfect place for her concert. We brought in a stage, a PA system, a spotlight, and got ready for the show. Edith Massey was from Baltimore, as was her band, Edie and the Eggs.

We put Edith up at a hotel, and the Eggs stayed at my place in Beverly Glen. The shows went great. Edith strutted around the stage in a black leather catsuit that laced up the sides, leaving a lot of skin showing, spewing lines like, "Hey, you punks, get off my lawn!" It was hilarious. The drummer in the Eggs was Gina Schock, a blue-collar Catholic school girl whose father was a stevedore on the docks in Baltimore.

Gina and I hit it off right away. And why not? She looked like Hanna Schygulla, Fassbinder's star, was really funny, had great meter, and hit hard, which was unusual for a female drummer. Her Dundalk accent was so thick I could hardly understand a word she said, but I didn't care. "Oil" came out as "ul"; my name, Steve, came out as "Stv." I was constantly saying, "What?"

After Gina returned to Baltimore, I called and suggested she come back out to Los Angeles, as the music scene was taking off here. To my surprise, Gina took me up on it. Her mother, who I came to know and like, said to her, "I bet he's a Jew." Gina said, "Ma, his last name is Martin and he has red hair." Her mother said, "I still think he's a Jew." She was correct. In early 1979, Gina drove across the country and moved in with me in Beverly Glen. With her drum kit and PA in the living room, we set off to find her a band.

One night I took her to see Werner Herzog's masterpiece *Aguirre, the Wrath of God*. She was silent during the screening, and when it was over and the lights came up, she turned to me, her eyes as big as saucers, and quietly said, "That movie makes me feel like stabbing someone."

I started taking Gina around to the new music clubs that were springing up all over LA. At Club 88, a run-down former piano bar on Pico in West LA, we saw the Go-Go's. Unlike most of the other new bands at that time, who were more or less punk-based, the Go-Go's were something else altogether. A female rock group playing their own songs with a sort of pumped-up sixties surf-and-rock sound, the Go-Go's were unique. Sitting in Club 88 watching the Go-Go's, I told Gina we should get her in a band like that.

And in a very short period of time, Gina wasn't in a band like the Go-Go's; she was in the Go-Go's. And they were on their way.

Enter the Baltimore Dynamo

Steven Martin, Culver City, California

Punk Rock Debutante

Jane Wiedlin,
Big Island,
Hawaii

Gina Schock, girl drummer, had just moved to Hollywood. The Go-Go's needed a girl drummer. And just like that, the random convergence of two things changed the future of music.

It was 1979. We met Gina at a beach party and made a date to get together at her new home in Beverly Glen. Gina lived in an old ramshackle hippie house, a leftover from the sixties. This was before that neighborhood became fancy-schmancy Beverly Hills–Adjacent. Her kit was set up in her living room, and we prepared to "jam." (Ha-ha, we NEVER would have used that word!) By the time we were thirty seconds into the first two-minute song, we were all grinning wildly at one another. This chick could PLAY. This chick SLAYED.

We left her place later, talking on top of one another, talking a mile a minute. She was PERFECT . . . except . . . she looked like someone from Three Dog Night . . . or Black Oak Arkansas . . . or Grand Funk Railroad . . . or any number of three-word seventies bands. We were punk rockers, and our sworn enemies were HIPPIES! Still, the way she pounded those drums! Underneath that huge blond ball of frizzy perm and her unpunk glasses, a cute little pixie was hiding. I announced that I could fix her. That I was gonna fix her. She was too amazing to let slip through our fingers. So we asked her if she wanted to be a Go-Go, and she said, "YES!"

The next part was trickier. Would she agree to a major makeover? Luckily, the answer was a resounding "FUCK YEAH!"

Turns out, she liked the way we looked and wanted to fit in. So, a trip to the drugstore to buy some cheap, probably toxic blue-black hair dye. The kind that was permanent, of course. There was no turning back. Back at home, I slopped on the dye. It turned her neck and ears black in the process, but hey, beauty is pain.

After that came the chop. In those days, we weren't real fussy about going to real hairdressers. I'd cut my own hair in the past, with varying results. How hard could it be? So, I proceeded to hack away a couple of pounds of perm-fried, formerly yellow hair . . . and voila!

Presenting the Punk Rock Debutante of 1979, Miss Regina Ann Schock!

This is Really Happening

The Go-Go's were up and running. After my first show, it really started to sink in that I was officially in the band. We began practicing on a regular basis at our home away from home, the Masque. I started to see a change in everyone pretty quickly. Week by week you could hear the improvement. Charlotte and Jane were bringing in a lot of new songs, and their writing was getting better and better. We were starting to really come into ourselves as musicians and songwriters. It wasn't just about playing for friends and a handful of fans anymore. It was evolving into something bigger, with our sights set on getting a manager and ultimately a record deal.

Ginger Canzoneri had the best taste in everything, from the way she dressed to her choices in music to the people she hung out with. She was by trade a graphic artist, and detail was important to her. You could also tell that she had good business sense by just one conversation with her. We had seen Ginger around the scene and had spoken with her several times. From those conversations, we knew she was interested in working with us, and we were certainly open to the idea. We weren't sure what her role would be, but we wanted her involved with us in some way. Each one of us individually and as a group connected with her, and she became our manager. At various shows, you would see her counting the money at the door and then usually talking with a club owner.

Barbie is a Friend of Mine

Belinda Carlisle,
Bangkok, Thailand

None of us had any money. I went from job to job in the early days. I would cash my checks and put all my money in a Barbie thermos. It seemed like a smart place to keep it. Disgraceland was the name of the house where I lived, and I would never leave my money there. It was kind of a flophouse, and it was known for being one of the dirtiest places to live in Hollywood. There was always a lot going on. People in and out all of the time. A couple could be having sex in one of the bedrooms while there was a fist-fight happening in the living room. Our friends were really interesting, to say the least.

When night came, we would venture out in search of the best party, wherever that may have been. There was always something happening in Chinatown. It was special because all the clubs were in the same square. One big hangout. We traveled as a group, and over the course of the evening you could find us at Hong Kong Café, Madame Wong's, or Cathay de Grande. We played at all three clubs regularly, and there were usually three different shows going on at the same time. While we were performing, I never left the Barbie thermos in the dressing room. I would bring it onstage with me and put it in Gina's kick drum. Nobody could get to it without my seeing them. I wouldn't let it out of my sight because all the money I had in the world was in there, and it was usually around a hundred dollars.

After we finished our shows, we would hang out in the plaza and then walk over to this bar that was like a throwback of Chinatown in the 1930s. It was ornately deco-rated, and we marveled at how cool it was. So gorgeous. Everyone's favorite drinks were Singapore Slings and Kamikazes. We'd talk about the crazy things that happened when we were playing that night. There is a show I won't forget that was at Cathay de Grande. I thought we had only one set, and someone offered me a quaalude. Of course I took it, not realizing we had two shows to do that night. Before long, it hit me, and I was immediately fucked up. I had to get it together enough to make it to the stage, where I sat in a chair, slumped over, slurring every word. That wasn't one of my finer moments. I made it through the second set, and no one complained. Our audience loved it. And they cheered me on as I barely kept my eyes open. Back then we weren't trying to be anything we weren't. The essence of the Go-Go's is that there really is no pre-tense. For us it was just a party. We were out there to have a good time. If you didn't time your drugs right, you just dealt with it.

At the end of the night, everybody went home with whomever. I always went home with Barbie.

KUSF 90.3 fm announces...

at the

OLD WALDORF

X & THE BLASTERS

tuesday jan 13, wednesday jan 14

GO-GO'S

friday jan 23

WALL OF VOODOO

& HUMAN HANDS

friday jan 30

100.9fm KTIM's DRASTIC PLASTIC announces...

D.N.A. & SNAKEFINGER sat jan 17

CAPT. BEEFHEART sat jan 24

Ginger was really something, and we were so impressed with her love of music and her love of our band.

By then we were playing several shows a week and getting a pretty decent following bouncing around from the Starwood to Club 88 to Hong Kong Cafe to Whisky a Go Go. It was around this time that we became the house band there. The Doors had once held that title. This was an important step for us moving forward as a band. The club had a very loyal following. Mario Maglieri, the owner of the Whisky and the Rainbow, was a handsome, affable gent that I had many conversations with over the years. I considered him a friend. He was quite a cool fellow. From night to night, the bands and the audience were very different. One of the things that was extraordinary about the Whisky was that there were a lot of out-of-town groups performing there, especially ones from the UK. Since the Go-Go's were the house band, we opened for many of them, which brings me to Madness. They were a ska band from the UK who were getting pretty big over there and in the rest of Europe. We were really excited to be opening for them. They were extremely cute with their British accents, button-fly Levi's, Doc Martens boots, and Fred Perry polo shirts. When we finished our shows and spent a couple of evenings together, there were some mad crushes going on.

Madness was heading back to the UK to prepare for their upcoming tour in 1980. Our managers were in frequent contact, figuring out how to get us over there. We wanted to continue our long-distance romances, only up close. The boys were spreading the word about the Go-Go's. The Specials, another UK ska band, were on their way to Los Angeles and booked at the Whisky. Madness and the Specials were both ska bands, but their approach was different. The music of Madness has a more mainstream pop affinity. The Specials are more hardcore ska, which attracts that kind of crowd. I remember watching them and thinking that every song had a razor-sharp edge to it. Their music and onstage presence were aggressive. They demonstrated what their audience was feeling.

The news came through! Our shows were booked, and we were preparing to leave for England. Ginger had worked everything out, and the schedule was set for us to open for Madness and the Specials on their seaside tours. We all gave up our living spaces and found places to park our cars until we returned. Ginger pawned many of her possessions, along with using money we had earned from doing shows, to buy airline tickets and make the necessary arrangements to get us settled in London until the Madness tour began. We packed our bags, said our goodbyes, and got on the now-defunct Laker Airways. This was the cheapest LA-to-London flight on the market. The minute we got to our seats in the last row of the airplane, we ordered drinks and lit up our cigarettes. During the flight, we were loud and disruptive until we got loaded enough to fall asleep. What a bunch of goofs, but what a lot of fun we had, always taking the party wherever we went.

Three days after our arrival, we began the tour with Madness. You are always in a difficult position being the opening band. Very few people are there to see you. They are there to see the headliners. The crowd wanted to be dancing to ska, not to what they considered to be cream-puff punk. They didn't seem to have much respect for women playing their own instruments. There was a lot of spitting, bottle throwing, and "show us your tits" while performing. Many nights we walked off stage in tears. Some of us had boyfriends in the other band, and that really helped a lot emotionally. My guy was bassist Mark Bedford, and we were crazy about each other. Mark said from the first time he saw us play that we were going to be hugely successful. I now had a cute English boyfriend, and I never wanted the tour to end.

A week or so later, we started our tour with the Specials. Their crowd was intense, and it seemed like any minute someone was gonna jump onstage and destroy it. I felt especially bad for Belinda because she was up front. They would "gob" on you. She would walk off stage with spit dripping off her. So gross. It couldn't reach me because I was behind the drums. I just had to dodge anything that they got their hands on to throw at me. In the midst of all this insanity, romance once again happened. Jane had a relationship with Terry Hall, the lead singer of the Specials. The end result of that was the hit single "Our Lips Are Sealed." I secretly had a crush on the handsome, smartly dressed Lynval Golding. There was never a dull moment on that tour.

Our first single was "We Got the Beat," released in the UK by Stiff Records and imported to the States. We always figured that we'd make it over there before we made it back home. As it turned out, it was exactly the opposite. While we were on tour in England,

"We Got the Beat" was starting to become popular in the States. Clubs on the East and West Coasts were playing it like crazy. So good to go home! Ginger was receiving tons of calls to book the band. The offers were much bigger than any amounts of money we had ever made. "We Got the Beat" was really making a difference in the perception that the bookers had of our band. We were finally making enough money from our live shows that we didn't have to worry about having jobs anymore. Things were changing rapidly, and we were now in a different category, no longer dependent on any stream of income other than what the Go-Go's earned.

For some reason, Margot did not seem to want to be a part of the above strategy moving forward. I feel she was way more comfortable staying where we were and not that interested in broadening the sound of the band. She wanted to keep the sound of the band way more punk, but the rest of us were heading into whatever direction the songs took us, which happened to be more melodic. This was causing friction. The band kept doing shows together until Margot got sick. We were booked at the Whisky on New Year's Eve, and that was something that you didn't cancel. It was a very important gig, especially for a band in our position. We started to look for another bassist to fill in. Kathy Valentine filled that spot—what a stroke of luck. She was a gal from Austin, Texas, and a true musician. Austin is known for its music scene. Kathy knew she wanted to be a guitar player at a young age. Following that path led to her being in lots of bands, thereby honing her skills. By the time she got to Los Angeles, she was already a damn good player. I didn't think about it then, but there was much in common between us. We both were serious about music and came from somewhere else to a destination in search of our ultimate goal.

Kathy's band, the Textones, played the same clubs we did. She was a guitarist and songwriter in the band and had heard about the Go-Go's and saw us perform live. Charlotte met Kathy at the Whisky one night, and they exchanged information letting her know Margot was sick and we had shows to do. The problem was Kathy played guitar, not bass. She borrowed a bass from one of her friends. Then Charlotte dropped off a rehearsal tape and Kathy got to work right away, as she had less than a week to learn all the songs. Quite a task, but she did it. Not only did Kathy learn the songs very quickly, but she also had a great feel for the bass, and *our* playing together was pretty tight considering this was brand-new for her and I. It's about timing. It's about feel. It's about eye contact. Once those elements lock in together, the foundation that makes it all work is achieved. Kathy fit in better than any of us could have hoped for. The audience loved our new addition, and so did we. To add to the excitement of the evening, John Belushi showed up. We got to hang out and talk with him after the show. Kathy and I became friends with John. We would contact each other whenever he was in LA or we were in New York. He was obviously very talented, and also a man who was deeply soulful, kind, and generous. Boy did he love music. The last time I saw him was at a Police show. We were all in the backstage area of the Forum. His wife Judy and his dear friend Dan Aykroyd were accompanying him. I walked over to speak with John and it was obvious how messed up he was. He was barely coherent. One week later he was dead. Hard to believe. It still doesn't seem real. What a tragic loss. Bless you John Belushi.

After the New Year's Eve show, it became apparent to the band that Kathy was going to replace Margot. The question was, who was going to tell her? Nobody wanted to be that person. We did feel bad about having to let her go. But it was absolutely the right thing to do in taking the band to the next level. Ginger was our manager, and we felt she should be the one to let Margot know. That happened exactly six days after the Whisky show. We immediately started rehearsals with Kathy, as we had several shows booked for the rest of the month. The final piece of the puzzle was intact and there was no stopping us.

Growing Up with the Go-Go's

Relah Eckstein, Tarzana, California

In the seventies, I majored in photography at Reseda High School and studied with H. Warren King, who was well-known and respected for teaching students how to "see." Mr. King would also take groups of kids to Europe in the summer for month-long photo tours and critique our work along the way. It was a crash course in photojournalism.

When I was seventeen years old, I got a fake ID and a part-time job at the Sherman Theatre in Sherman Oaks, California. This is where I met Steve Martin, who was the head projectionist, and we hit it off. We both liked weird films, drinking, smoking pot, and punk rock. Steve was really smart, fun, and ambitious. He also worked at the Nuart Theatre and set up an evening of performances with Edith Massey, the star of John Waters's *Pink Flamingos*, and her all-girl punk rock band, Edie and the Eggs. This is how I met Gina.

Gina was the cutest and coolest of the Eggs, and I liked her and her Baltimore accent right away. She totally stood out to me. We became good friends and started hanging out a lot. I spent more time with her than I did at home, running all over LA taking photographs everywhere we went.

In August 1979, I went to San Francisco with the Go-Go's. We loaded everything up in Gina's truck, and it turned out to be quite an interesting trip. The band played two nights at Mabuhay Gardens. We all stayed at Alison Saracena's apartment. She was a friend of Gina's, who she met the year before when she played there with Edie. Alison was a great host, and I took color photos of the girls clowning around and getting ready for the concert.

The first night went well, but the second night had problems. I ate mushrooms and couldn't find the truck. We all went in search of it and eventually found the truck only blocks away. Jane and I rode in the back with all the equipment and suitcases piled on top of one another. It wasn't very comfortable, and things kept sliding around. I took color photos of Jane wearing a cowboy hat, white boots, and red jacket, and she took a photo of me looking at the road. What a crazy dangerous thing to be doing, driving down Route 1 on mushrooms.

When we got back to LA, we went shopping on quaaludes in Hollywood. Gina bought a two-hundred-dollar pair of leather pants, and we got tattoos at Cliff Raven's on the Sunset Strip. Gina got drum notes on her left wrist, and I got a little spider on my right wrist. Jane wanted an X on her ear, but at that time they wouldn't tattoo above your neck, so she didn't get one. My tattoo cost ten dollars.

It sure was fun meeting Gina when I was eighteen, taking photos, hanging out, going to lots of shows, and growing up with the Go-Go's. I was very shy, and they were relaxed and liked to goof around. My dad would tell his friends they were good, responsible young girls who had a band. My mom told me later that she prayed for me every night. The Go-Go's are my favorite band. I love their music, and I felt part of it. The music you listen to when you're growing up is always the most important music.

JANUARY 1980

S	M	T	W	T	F	S
She was heartbreakingly beautiful as the legendary French courtesan in *Camille*. But what was Greta Garbo's own native land?	~~Robbed~~ New Year's Eve	**1** New Year's Day	**2** *Starwood*	**3**	**4** Club 88	**5**
6	**7**	**8**	**9** *Starwood*	**10**	**11**	**12**
13 Alison's B-day	**14**	**15** Martin Luther King's Birthday	**16**	**17**	**18** Hong Kong	**19**
20	**21** Dad's B-day	**22**	**23**	**24** ~~Starwood~~	**25** San Francisco Johnny's B-day	**26**
27 Santa Cruz	**28**	**29**	**30**	**31**		

58

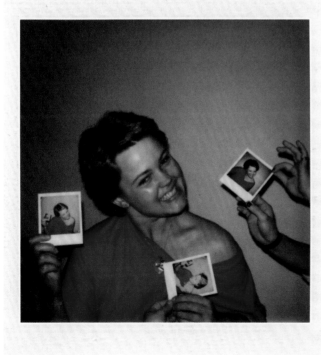

Van "81"

Aren't **We** the Lucky Ones

Bands that played at the Roxy usually had record deals. It was definitely industry heavy as far as clubs go. We had two important shows booked there on January 30 and 31, 1981. Ginger was making this an event and wanted every label in town to know about our shows. ABC News was there one night interviewing and filming us. Prior to this, people came more for the scene and to party with the band. This time they weren't there just to see "a band"; they were there to see the Go-Go's and were hanging on every word that came out of our mouths. Lots of fan participation with many shout-outs of "Belinda, we love you!" I could see our audience changing and becoming more mainstream.

Ginger had been speaking to many record labels. One in particular kept coming back, and that was Miles Copeland's label, I.R.S. Records, a subsidiary of A&M Records. They certainly weren't your typical corporate label. Going into the offices and getting to know folks working there was very comfortable. They seemed to be people like us. We were all on a first-name basis. Ultimately, we signed with I.R.S. on April Fool's Day, 1981. We couldn't wait to get to the East Coast to begin rehearsing and making our first record. We started recording that album, *Beauty and the Beat*, on April 10. Miles pushed hard for producer Richard Gottehrer to do our record. Richard was a great songwriter and producer with a lengthy track record of hits. He was a jokester loaded with positive energy.

He knew how to take our songs and make adjustments where needed, getting them as close to a hit record as one could. The rest was up to fate. We followed his lead and wound up making a historic album. Miles had chosen wisely.

The months that we spent in New York City making that record were full of sex, drugs, and drinking. Just about every night after recording we would go out clubbing. One thing would lead to another. When you're in your early twenties and suddenly dropped into prepping for rock stardom, the transition is adventurous and exciting. You go from living on practically no money to a weekly per diem, getting everything paid for, and staying in a hotel. We were having the time of our lives. In fact, it was more than making a record. For the band, it was the beginning of a big change that was about to happen, and we were starting to feel like we really mattered. The possibility of being a rock star became the probability. It wasn't just a dream anymore.

Richard was easy to work with, and he had so many great stories he would pass on to us every day. I would try anything he asked me to do because I knew I would learn from him even if we didn't wind up recording what he suggested. We would work on a song until we exhausted all efforts to improve it. Not every song needed to be deconstructed. Most were pretty together. Making *Beauty and the Beat* went really smoothly, and he helped me to understand the songwriting process much more. Whether you start out with a guitar or a vocal melody or just some lyrics, I was understanding how to put a song together. Of course, at this point I had no idea the difference in a paycheck for someone who was a songwriter in a band and for someone who was just a member of the band. What a difference. Enough to break up most bands, and in several years, it did exactly that.

It was the end of May, and we had completed the album. We would miss New York City and all that went with it, but it was time to head back to the West Coast to begin rehearsals for our summer tour. The tour started in June and would continue through the end of the year. Our transportation for most of it was in a twelve-seater van. *This* is paying your dues. Driving from city to city, state to state, every day settling in a different location. It wasn't easy, but the crowds were getting bigger and bigger, and we were thrilled. In Cherry Hill, New Jersey, getting ready to play, we got the wonderful news!

Family Portrait

Ten Takes and a Pizza Break

Charlotte Caffey,
Los Angeles,
California

After years of playing gigs and being rejected by every major label, the Go-Go's met on April 1, 1981, at Kelbo's, a landmark Los Angeles tiki-themed restaurant, to sign with Miles Copeland's I.R.S. Records. The next day we all jetted off to New York to record our first album, *Beauty and the Beat*.

It was a beautiful spring day as I nervously walked from the Wellington Hotel on Fifty-Fifth and Seventh to Penny Lane Studios on Nineteenth and Fifth for the first day of recording. Entering the studio, I was really aware that this was not a demo session but the *real* thing.

I felt fortunate to be working with veteran producer Richard Gottehrer, who was also a songwriter, having co-written such classics as "My Boyfriend's Back" and "I Want Candy." As a very young kid, I was obsessed with listening to my transistor radio. The biggest stations in Los Angeles were KHJ and KRLA, which both played the extremely diverse pop music of the 1960s. These songs became my refuge.

Richard had a lot of energy and tons of patience. He had his hands full with this hilarious ragtag, punky group of girls with their hangovers and opinions. But he really took us seriously and listened to everyone's ideas, giving equal focus to each girl.

I recall singing background vocals in the bathroom at the studio. The acoustics were really great because of the tiled floor and walls, but there was also a row of urinals that smelled like mothballs! The result were vocals that sparkled and sounded like post-punk Shangri-Las. And about a week into the sessions, I made a decision to record all my guitar parts with one pick. That pick lives in a frame on my studio wall.

One of Richard's most radical suggestions was slowing down tempos so that the listener could understand the lyrics and let the melodies breathe. The songs were played really fast and furious onstage, and I thought that the band would sound wimpy if we played too slow. Being a team player, I begrudgingly went along with it. And when it came time to record "We Got the Beat," all it took was ten tries and a pizza break. Number eleven became the Go-Go's lucky number.

I didn't understand at the time, but Richard really knew how to make records that would sound great on the radio. He also had so much respect for songwriting and taught me how to emphasize and exploit the best aspects of each song. It was like being in a master class. And eventually I realized that he was so right about those damn tempos!

When I got my first copy of *Beauty and the Beat*, I carefully opened it, inhaled that distinct new-record smell, looked at the pictures and credits, and read the liner notes. This was the ritual I performed whenever I would get a new record—only this time it was my band and my album!

From the grooves to the tube

GO·GO'S

WATCH THE

**SATURDAY NIGHT LIVE
SATURDAY NOV. 14
11:30pm ON CHANNEL 4**

**WITH SPECIAL GUEST HOST,
BERNADETTE PETERS**

**ALBUM, CASSETTE, & SINGLE
AVAILABLE ON I.R.S. RECORDS**

YOU'LL SEE 'EM. NOW BUY 'EM.

Telegram

TIB139(1242)(4-014875S318)PD 11/14/81 1237

ICS IPMRNCZ CSP

2138744853 TDRN LOS ANGELES CA 13 11-14 1237P EST

PMS NBC SATURDAY NIGHT LIVE ATTN GINGER CANZONERI AND THE GO-GOS RPT

DLY MGM, DLR 9 PM, DLR

30 ROCKERFELLER PLZ

NEW YORK NY 10112

I LOVE YOU GOOD LUCK AND I LL BE WATCHING TONIGHT SEE YOU SOON

PEE-WEE HERMAN

NNNN

W.U. 1201-SF (R5-69)

The Rolling Stones wanted us to open for them two days later in Rockford, Illinois. We were over the moon, incredibly excited, and about to meet living legends.

We moved a couple of shows around, and before we knew it we were doing a sound check on the same stage that the Rolling Stones would be playing on later that evening. I made friends with their road crew and got to sit on Charlie Watts's drum kit and play a little during sound check. I remember his tech telling me that the drums were worth a pittance compared to the value of the rug they sat on. That is so Charlie Watts. Mick Jagger was doing his laps around the arena before the show started. Ronnie Wood and Keith Richards were having drinks, so Charlie and Bill Wyman came over to say hi. Not too long after doing a show with them, Kathy and I did wind up hanging out with Ronnie and his then wife Jo quite a bit in New York. I was so knocked out to be standing on the side of the stage watching the Stones perform that close up. Opening for the Stones was the thrill of a lifetime. I will carry it with me always.

The following week, we did three sold-out nights at the Greek Theatre in Los Angeles. Pee-wee Herman was our MC for those evenings. Paul Reubens was a new face in town at the time. I don't think the audience really knew what to make of him, but we loved it. He was brilliant. A very gifted actor and comedian. Not long after he did our shows, he had quite the success with *Pee-wee's Playhouse*. He also did several films—always smart, always clever. What a super swell guy. The following week, we left for New York to do several in-store appearances and more press for our UK/European tour. In-store appearances were always exhausting, but we did love to meet our crazy fans. We arrived in England, did five shows, and then went on to Amsterdam, Paris, and Berlin for more concerts and press promoting *Beauty and the Beat*. We flew from Germany back to New York City on November 12, and two days later we played for millions watching us on *Saturday Night Live*. Back then, that show was a hugely influential selling tool for a band. Remember when we used to wait all week to see who would be on that weekend? After we played, the following week's sales spiked and we started selling hundreds of thousands of records.

Just when things were great, they got a little better. We got a call from Miles asking if we would like to open for the Police on their US and European *Ghost in the Machine* tour.

Oh wow!

GOING TO THE GO-GO'S
WITH THE ROLLING STONES OCT. 1

Metro Rockford Ill.
10/8/81

ROCKFORD

ARTIST

ANDY + MAMA 1/10/82

AMSTERDAM AIRPORT 1/10/82

Miles was the older brother of Stewart Copeland, the drummer in the Police. The other brother, Ian Copeland, was the head of their booking agency, F.B.I. You gotta love it . . . I.R.S., F.B.I., and the Police. Our music had much in common with them. If you went to a Police show, you were probably going to end up singing and dancing with every song. That is exactly what our audience did. What a smart combination. All three members of the band were gentlemen, even going so far as to bring us champagne when our record went to number 1 while on tour with them. Sting was such an impressive songwriter and singer. Stewart and Andy Summers were great musicians and songwriters as well. What a supergroup. What a band. After the Go-Go's finished our set every night, you could usually find me at the side of the stage watching the Police. It was hard to take my eyes off of Stewart when he was drumming. We had a fabulous time touring with the guys, playing eighteen-to-twenty-thousand-seat arenas. We couldn't wait for our chance to perform as headliners at those same venues. And that did happen soon after we finished our tour with the Police.

86

KISS AT SOLID GOLD
Dec. 7th "81"

ANDY GIBB
"SOLID GOLD"   Dec 9th

Big head + Kathy

DANCER
SOLID GOLD

InStore / Boston Aug 81

Boston

10/2/81

O'Hare Chicago

Airport to Miami

91

Chrissie Hynde
Sept. 81

Kathy / Pete FARNDON / Jane / Charlotte

Martin Chambers / Peggy Sue Scott / Jimi Scott

Nov. 81 Paris, Hotel Baltimore

Miles "thoughtful" Copeland

Airport/Miami

Miles + Mary House
Nov. 81

Miles House

DATE	VENUE	HOTEL
SUN. 9/27	Seattle, Washington Eagle Auditorium (1200)	Park Hilton 206-464-1980
MON. 9/28	Bellingham, Washington Viking Union Lounge (800)	Best Western Key Motel 206-733-4060
TUES. 9/29	Vancouver, B. C. Commodore Ballroom (1000)	Century Plaza 604-687-0575
WED. 9/30	Travel day to Rockford, Illinois, via Chicago	Clock Tower Inn 815-398-6000
THUR 10/1	*Stones Show* *ROCKFORD, Ill.*	Clock Tower Inn 815-398-6000
FRI. 10/2	Travel day to San Fran- cisco, via Chicago *6:00pm*	Holiday Inn 415-626-6103
SAT. 10/3	San Francisco, Cal. Market St. Cinema	Holiday Inn 415-626-6103
SUN. 10/4	Santa Cruz, Cal. The Catalyst	Best Western 408-426-7575
MON. 10/5	Santa Barbara, Cal. The Arlington Theatre	Travel Lodge 805-965-8527
TUES. 10/6	*Mike Douglas Show* *Accountant 10:00 AM.*	HOJO *MARK* 213-980-8000
WED. 10/7	*OFF YEAH!*	*OFF*
THUR. 10/8	Los Angeles, Cal The Greek Theatre	

9/10th The Greek

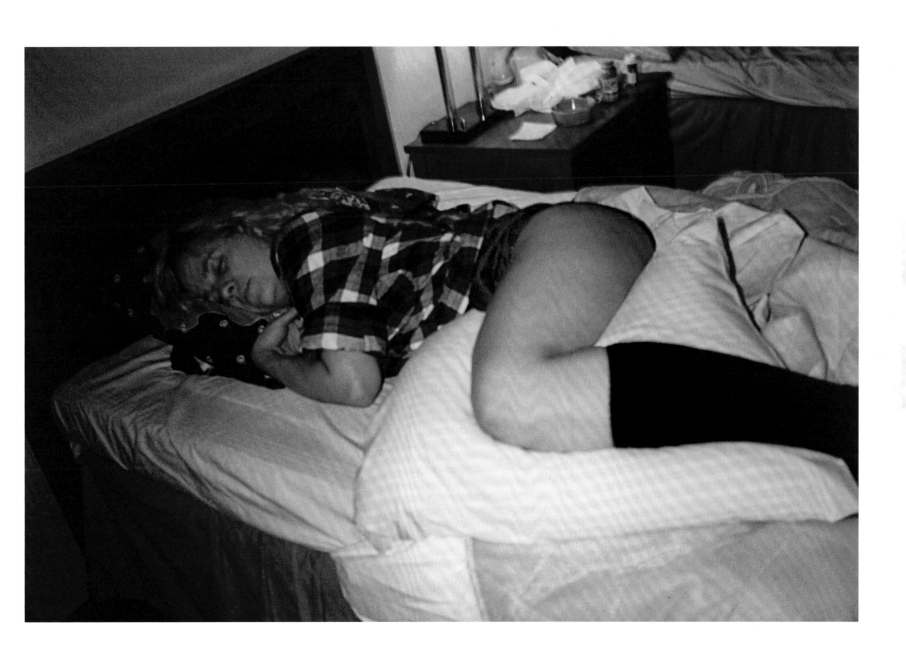

CLUB FOOT
Presents I.R.S. Recording Artists

THE GO·GO'S
& BIG BOYS

THURSDAY SEPT. 10

TICKETS $5.00 at: INNER SANCTUM
ZEBRA ON LAVACA
MUSIC EXPRESS
CLUB BOX OFFICE

The Top 100 album: Beauty & the Beat
The hit single: Our Lips Are Sealed

I.R.S.

© 1981 r. luckett
for ooh!ship
WE LOVE YOU KATHY!

LONE ☆ STAR
PRINTING Co.

Go-Go's Ascending

Richard Luckett,
Austin, Texas

Austin, Texas, September 10, 1981: *Oh, those girls!* The excitement in Club Foot was palpable that Thursday night long ago, but—forty years later—I can still remember it like it was yesterday. My friend and our Austin homegirl Kathy Valentine was about to take the stage with her band the Go-Go's at *our* club—and we couldn't be more excited or happier for her. *Beauty and the Beat* had dropped just weeks before in July; myself and my best friend and venue manager Brad First had watched with delight as it began its slow, inexorable climb up the *Billboard* Top 100 . . . We simply had no doubt that it would go to number 1, which it eventually did, on March 6, 1982.

That night, *Beauty and the Beat* was at number 44, and as far as the Austin market was concerned, Brad and I (as house DJs) were doing our very best to assist by putting the LP in heavy rotation at the club—their single "We Got the Beat" filled our dance floor *without fail*. At that time I was also doing a lot of the posters for the venue, and of course I did this poster and dedicated it to Kathy, and *of course* the show was sold out. So, there were Brad and I, perched high up in the DJ booth—grinning from ear to ear—as Belinda, Jane, Kathy, Gina, and Charlotte took the stage to thunderous applause from an adoring Austin crowd. Gina counted off, then slammed into the drum intro to "Skidmarks on My Heart," bashing those tubs for all she was worth. I don't believe I saw five bigger smiles on that stage . . . and Kathy's was the biggest of all. Yes, the first Go-Go's show in Austin was absolutely fucking transcendent, and the rest, as they say, was hist— I mean *her*story.

SOLD OUT!

THE

GO-GO'S

THE

GO-GO's

OCT. 8·10

GREEK THEATRE

COLBY POSTER PRINTING CO., 1332 W. 12th Pl. L.A. 90015

In the early evening of October 8, 1981, I was excitedly driving my dark green Datsun B210 through Hollywood on my way to the Greek Theatre. I'd been asked by the Go-Go's to introduce them at their debut there. Even though my relationship with them consisted mostly of saying hi after one of their string of early shows, I felt like we were friends.

I loved every single thing about the Go-Go's—their energy, their personas, and especially their music. I admired that they were wild rebels and had cool underground street cred. At the same time, they seemed enormously commercial, and I always thought it was plain as day that they'd become gigantically famous. My early career paralleled the beginnings of the Los Angeles punk scene. I knew Exene Cervenka from when we both lived in Florida, and when she came to California and met John Doe, I became a groupie to their band, X. Gary Panter, the designer of *The Pee-wee Herman Show*, was the preeminent illustrator of punk band posters. I loved the early punk scene and felt an affinity with many of the bands.

Back to my obsession with the Go-Go's. I'd seen one of their earliest shows at the Masque and fell in love. That was one of the great qualities about the band: You fell in love with them during their performances. It was impossible not to. I felt like they had everything, that they were as close to perfect as you could get.

When they asked me to introduce their shows at the Greek, I was absolutely thrilled. I was working on a TV show that was being produced by Steve Martin, and one of the segments I was writing was about female felons. I wanted him to see the Go-Go's so that maybe they could be part of this women's penitentiary piece. To my surprise, he said he'd come with me!

My plan was to arrive just before going onstage, so I was driving through Hollywood in my Pee-wee suit with Steve Martin in the passenger seat. I'm carrying precious cargo, and I'm on my way to do something I was wildly excited about.

I glided my Datsun into the super VIP, backstage artist entrance like I was entering the Bat Cave. In 1981, to arrive somewhere with Steve Martin was like showing up with Elvis. We walked from my parking spot into the backstage area and into the greenroom, where the Go-Go's were relaxing and getting ready to do their show.

I tried my best to be nonchalant as I introduced Steve to the band. After a couple of minutes, a stage manager escorted Steve and me to the backstage wing. I could see out into the audience from where we were standing and heard the audience react as the lights dimmed. Six thousand people screamed in the darkness and cheered as I walked out to the middle of the stage. When the lights came up on me, the audience booed. They were expecting to see the band, and instead they got me. I wasn't really known yet, so the majority of the people had no idea who I was. I introduced myself and launched into my very short 'act'—pulling weird toys out of a paper bag and laughing as I demonstrated what I thought was funny about each one.

Evidently, the audience didn't think my toys were as funny as I did, since they started throwing hot dogs onto the stage. I could see Steve Martin standing in the wings watching me. It was very surreal.

I wisely cut my routine short and yelled out into the darkness, "Ladies and gentleman, here they are . . . the Go-Go's!!!"

NATIONAL ACADEMY OF RECORDING ARTS & SCIENCES

I take great pleasure in congratulating you on your Grammy nomination. This honor has been conferred upon you by the voting members of the Recording Academy who are your fellow creators and craftsmen. Within a few weeks you will receive a nominations plaque.

Grammy winners will be announced on the 24th Annual Grammy Awards telecast over CBS-TV on Wednesday, February 24, 1982, emanating live from the Shrine Auditorium in Los Angeles. You are cordially invited to attend the telecast, and a buffet party at the Biltmore Hotel immediately following, as our guest. This invitation is non-transferable.

Please note that because of time limitations not all Grammy Awards will be presented on the telecast. You will be notified if the category in which you are nominated is one of those selected to be announced on the telecast. The remaining categories will be awarded immediately before going on the air, and the winners who are present will be video-taped accepting their awards for tape insertion in the live telecast. There will be no substitute acceptors for absent nominees.

Some Recording Academy chapters in other cities are planning non-televised Grammy Awards celebrations on the same night; if you would like more information, please check the appropriate space on your reply card.

Very truly yours,
NATIONAL BOARD OF TRUSTEES

By: Bill Ivey, National President

BI/sw
24A1

© NARAS

GO-GO's

Has been nominated in the Twenty-Fourth Annual Grammy Awards for:

1981

In the category of:

BEST NEW ARTIST

Vacation
in the Video Age

We were doing a great job at handling everything the record company was throwing at us, even though we were being pushed to the limit. Youth does have its advantages. The tours were unending but we were happy to be on the road promoting the worldwide release of our first album. On our itinerary when it said "day off" it was never really a day off. Instead, it would be press all day and into the evening—in-person interviews, phone interviews, and perhaps another record store appearance. And then there was TV. Not a lot of time to think about all that was happening to us in a relatively short period of time.

I was really excited about our Grammy nomination considering it had only been a couple years since I was living in Baltimore only dreaming that something like this might one day happen to me. Dressed up in our fabulous thrift store outfits (hadn't made any real money yet), we all arrived at the Shrine Auditorium. Along with our plus-ones, we filled a whole row, with Ginger leading the pack. Fortunately, the Best New Artist category was up first. When the winner was announced, everybody in the band looked at one another in disbelief. Sheena Easton? Our entire row stood up and walked out, heading for the lobby. During the commercial break, we watched as they scurried around trying to fill in the ten empty seats. We were laughing as we got into our limos heading to Chasen's for our "victory party." In our minds, we were the Best New Artist of 1981.

Vacation, our second album, was put together pretty quickly. We had one week in February to rest before starting rehearsals. Eager to capture the same chemistry we had with the first album, we asked Richard Gottehrer to work with us again. This time we recorded at Indigo Ranch. The recording studio was nestled in the hills of Malibu and felt like a getaway from the madness of LA. After playing on the road for a year and a half straight, we were now entering the studio feeling more like pros. Exhausted from nonstop touring but still absolutely delighted with the success of the first record.

As we were putting songs together for the new record, Kathy showed Charlotte one that she had written a couple of years earlier. Charlotte thought it was a great song that needed some work on the chorus. They fine-tuned it and then brought it to us at rehearsals. That song was "Vacation." I loved the story and what it was about. The chord progressions and the vocal melody were great. It felt like a summer anthem. People thought of us as a fun party band. The song was classic Go-Go's. The only thing was, Kathy wasn't sure about the first line of the song and asked Jane if she had any thoughts on it. Off the top of her head she said, "Can't seem to get my mind off of you." Another hit song was finished and radio ready.

MTV had launched the video for "Our Lips Are Sealed," which was the first single off *Beauty and the Beat*. People were very curious about this new music cable network, and it was having a huge impact on record sales for various artists. MTV was a game changer for the record business in 1981. There were some shiny new faces on that network that we soon got to know. They were called VJs, a new term for all of us. The Go-Go's had been interviewed by all five of the initial VJs that worked there. They seemed to love music and there was an excitement in their voices when they spoke about a band and the video we were about to see. Martha Quinn always stuck out to me. She looked like she could be a member of the Go-Go's with her short cute pixie haircut. And she had girlish charm, which sort of made her fit in with us even more. Not to mention she was great at her job.

Music delivered to the general public in that format from this new network made you feel like you were really getting to know the artists you were listening to. "Our Lips Are Sealed" was shot with part of a leftover budget from a big Police video. The second video for that album was another single, "We Got the Beat." It was taken from live concert footage recorded at Palos Verdes High School. I.R.S. was a small record label and didn't have large amounts of money for any of its acts. Fortunately, our first record generated tons of money for the company. The "Vacation" video would be our first real big-budget production, and we were ready for it.

Ginger was in England when she came across a postcard of women on water skis. The idea started to percolate in her head. As I have mentioned already, Ginger had impeccable taste and we knew she would come up with something visually stunning. Jay Boberg was the vice president of I.R.S. Records at the time. He had given Ginger a list of directors they thought would be perfect for the "Vacation" video. When she saw Mick Haggerty's name, she immediately knew he was right for the job. Previously, they had worked together when Mick and C.D. Taylor co-directed the *Totally Go-Go's* video. Two artsy English gentlemen, Mick and C.D. were such a cool creative team. C.D.'s approach was from that of a painter. Mick came from graphic design. What a smart combo.

The thought of the five of us wearing tutus on water skis was such a funny idea. We never wanted to be scantily clothed or in suggestive poses. It's just not who we were or what we were ever about. I think the scope of our work shows that. We always aired on the lighter side. Ginger's initial idea started to come to fruition when she handed Mick and C.D. the postcard. This reminded C.D. of a movie Elvis did called *Clambake*. The two of them watched it thinking it would work beautifully for the right visuals. *Clambake* was made using rear-screen projection, and now the guys were set on making it work for the "Vacation" video. Mick went to Cypress Gardens, Florida, with a cameraman to get the water-skiing footage. They found five performers that resembled our body types and size. The trip resulted in getting the stills for the album sleeve and the film footage of the water skiers. It was really starting to come together.

On June 5, 1982, the band arrived at A&M Studios in Hollywood. Although I.R.S. was our record label, our albums were distributed by A&M. The A&M complex included offices, recording studios, and the famous Chaplin soundstage. Charlie Chaplin is a hero of mine. This man was obviously a visionary. I love *The Tramp*, *The Kid*, *Modern Times*, and *The Great Dictator*. What wonderfully thoughtful commentaries on life—present and future. He also composed the music for his films. As I made my way through that historic soundstage, it was another memorable moment in my life that was granted by being in the Go-Go's.

The first shots of the day began with us sitting on our flight cases looking bored to tears. The second part of the shoot was the band in tutus supposedly water skiing

around a lake. This was done with the rear-screen projection method that Mick and C.D. had studied, and I was very fond of it as I am an old-movie buff. Individually and collectively, we stood in front of a screen holding on to ski ropes. By that time, we were exhausted and had already indulged in party favors. So when you see us skiing and looking as though we might fall over . . . that was kind of true. We were all a bit wasted and needed to get a little air, so we headed outside. Ginger began photographing all of us leaving the studio and walking onto La Brea. That must have been quite a scene. People probably thought we were crazy hookers traipsing around the streets of Hollywood in tutus. Maybe we did look like we were a little cracked, but regardless we were in the number one band in the country.

We began touring for the *Vacation* album, heading first to Hawaii and then back to California for a bunch of shows leading up to our appearance at the Hollywood Bowl. That venue has iconic status. The Beatles had played there in the sixties and Frank Sinatra in the forties, and many more artists of their stature. When I walked out to do our sound check, it looked so big, so vast. I was immediately intimidated, and those twenty thousand seats were empty! Playing Madison Square Garden, the Philadelphia Spectrum, and the Boston Garden was no small accomplishment for us. But this was special and the biggest show we had ever done in our hometown. That night, I never thought about being the first all-female rock band to play the Bowl. I still don't think about it until it's brought up. We do what we love to do and happen to be women. The record business was primarily run by men: The Go-Go's beat the odds.

An Impossible Task

Ginger Canzoneri,
West Hollywood,
California

Wrangling five young women, each with a very strong identity of self and their own often stubborn decision-making process, was a challenge. In the early days, my way of settling the band's nonsense disputes was to resort to corporal punishment. When the bickering started, I liked to grab them by their short punk hair and bang their heads together, which would always elicit laughter, making everyone giggle and quickly forget what they were arguing about. In later years, we learned to apply the rule of good sportsmanship. The girls were very good sports; they displayed a high level of trust by allowing me to dress them in towels and facial cream masks for their first album cover and water skis and tutus for their second album.

Decades later, I can honestly report not hearing any complaints, outbursts, crying, or demands that day during the filming of the band's video for their single "Vacation." I was present throughout, taking photos, because any direction you pointed your camera was too good a photographic opportunity to miss. It was an arduous day from sunup to sundown, with multiple stage setups and wardrobe changes.

My only solace that day was quick trips to my management office, located nearby in the historic Hollywood landmark known as Crossroads of the World. It was a good way to clear my mind and escape the hubbub and tedium of delay between stage setups. And I could gather some necessary distractions for the girls to help pass the time, like stacks of publicity photos and vinyl record albums begging for their autographs. They all really enjoyed this task and developed their own unique style with repeated signings. Jane Wiedlin cleverly used a special red ink marker when signing the *Beauty and the Beat* LP that matched the nail polish bottle on the floor near her foot on the front cover photo. A stroke of genius! I'm so pleased that I still have one of these in my collection.

The management office was a source of immense pride; it was one of the larger spaces available in the Crossroads complex, and in my mind the obvious, practical choice for an expanding company. Housed within my office was the Go-Go's Fan Club in their own dedicated space. The fan club office was constantly abuzz with activity, peals of laughter, and gasps at the tidal wave of fan mail that poured in daily. It was an exciting time; everything was running frenetically but on schedule.

When the film crew stopped for a stage change, it allowed the Go-Go's a well-deserved break. They headed for the nearest exit in the direction of Sunset Boulevard, all with the exception of Belinda. I followed along dutifully with my camera while they were walking, skipping, twirling, wearing their pink water-ski costumes. It was quite a sight as they showed off publicly on the streets of Hollywood, coming to rest on a convenient bus bench. It was late-afternoon sunlight, "the magic hour."

You can see a hint of exhaustion on their faces. But they soon perked up for the next fun round of filming with water-ski ropes. They worked late into the night, standing squished together onstage while images of moving surf and sea spray were projected on the screen behind them. There were fun moments. It was amusing—hysterical, actually—to watch as they hammed it up for the cameras, especially for their solo cameo shots. It was fortunate that the Go-Go's were big hams and loved to mug it up for any camera. That night there was a bit of healthy competition as they eyed, with obvious side glances, each other's performances in an effort to outdo one another. My girls were champs. They always delivered on cue.

Destination: Go-Go Land

Jodie Foster,
Los Angeles,
California

"The Go-Go's are coming out with us tonight." That was the plan my movie brother Rob Lowe was cooking up from his New York City hotel room. I had just flown in on a magazine's dime so Rob and I could share one of those night-on-the-town interviews, a kind of celebrity scavenger hunt in and out of Manhattan nightspots. It was 1983, and we were both young enough to make every Friday night count. "Kathy's so funny. And Gina, she's the drummer. Hilarious," he said. And they were. It was like an instant pajama party with those wild, mouthy girls, who were up for any dare. We all crammed into a car, picking up friends at various clubs and bars along the way hanging out the windows. Destination? Area, the super cool art imaginarium in the West Village. There were dancers in cages, human dioramas, taxidermy animals, and a unisex bathroom as big as a loft. It was one of those magical nights when you talk to strangers, lose your voice, and finally greet the sun as you all stumble outside the club looking for donuts. I can still remember Kathy's woodpecker laugh and Gina shouting, "Come on, shitpots," in that Baltimore twang.

Eventually I met Belinda, Jane, and Charlotte when the gang was recording in London. Dinner was at Mr. Chow's but segued out to god knows where. I remember dancing in some abandoned factory turned into a club, then ordering room service sandwiches and watching bad TV with a host of new friends who had also come along for the ride. Even though a few boyfriends or crushes got thrown into the Go-Go mix, the girls preferred a group-fun dynamic. Belinda was the troublemaker yet somehow managed to get away with everything. Jane floated behind with that dreamy sweetness. Charlotte seemed sensible but would disappear at the drop of a hat. Kathy and Gina were the goofy ones of the puppy pack, always competing for the "I can't believe she said that" award. When the girls were all together in one space, no one could get a word in. Even that first night in London I could feel their energy feed off one another and escalate depending on who was in the mood to take the helm.

From that night on, I became a permanent fixture of the Go-Go road show. I'd had a serious life as a child actress growing up. I was a good kid. School, work, responsibility. But I'd completely missed out on that adolescent spirit you can only get from people your own age. My college friends were more directed and careful. The Go-Go's felt alternately dangerous and familiar. They were up for edgy mischief but still loved their parents. They embraced the rock 'n roll lifestyle but showed up for people they loved. Being around those girls made me feel like I was really living for once. I was finally young and hanging out with the band. They had the beat, and that's exactly what I desperately wanted.

kroq-fm and wolf & rissmiller present

AT THE
HOLLYWOOD BOWL
AUGUST 29, 1982

"vacation" cassette and album on i.r.s. records

manufactured and distributed by a&m records, inc.

The "Get Up and Go" video I directed was shot in a space the size of a living room when it should have been the size of a basketball court.

The idea of the video was the Go-Go's via *Gumby*—live-action Go-Go's composited with stop-motion clay animation versions of themselves. It would be fun. My brother Steve, the producer, arranged to film in an abandoned public-access television studio in the Boston suburb of Somerville. On arrival from the West Coast, we discovered an exceptionally tiny studio with no blue seamless cove. A blue seamless cove was vital for filming the actual Go-Go's lip-synching, fake playing their instruments, and dancing for later compositing with stop-motion clay animation of miniature Go-Go's simultaneously being realized by animators the Chiodo Brothers in Burbank. My brother had the crew build a makeshift seamless cove out of foam core and duct tape and paint it blue. It was hillbilly crude, like a funky igloo. Worked perfectly.

In the middle of a grueling tour of sold-out arenas, the Go-Go's arrived at the studio beat and upbeat along with a drum set, electric guitars, and electric bass—they wanted to get the filming finished so they could prepare for that evening's performance at the sold-out Boston Garden. I explained what we were going to shoot and how and why. They said, "Okay, just tell us what to do."

Our first shot was a pullback from a screen-filling close-up of Belinda to reveal all the Go-Go's playing their instruments and singing. Cinematographer extraordinaire Frederick Elmes quickly and calmly rehearsed camera and dolly moves with the pickup crew in the tiny studio. The Go-Go's took their places on the crude seamless blue cove, audio playback rolled, filming began, Fred demonstrated his genius.

We shot the Go-Go's performing and dancing in a variety of combinations—my direction included the never-imagined line "You're dancing with a Gumby version of yourself. Action!"—all aligned with drawings on tracing paper taped over the video monitor that matched what I had given the animators. The Go-Go's were excellent, playing it straight and fun. After two hours, I crossed the last shot off the shot list and called it a wrap. In a flash the Go-Go's packed their stuff, told us we had tickets for that night's show, and split. We broke down the set and headed toward Boston Garden to see the Go-Go's perform and maybe get some chowder.

When we arrived mid-show, the Boston Garden fans were stomping, cheering, and screaming as the Go-Go's played songs from their two hit albums. I knew the band had fans, but I had no idea they got worked up like Beatles fans. Boston Garden was shaking like an earthquake; every song ended with the crowd roaring. A far cry from the postage stamp–size blue cove igloo in Somerville.

After the show while in the dressing room with the Go-Go's, we heard a commotion outside and figured something big must have just happened. Something big had just happened. The Go-Go's had just happened. Outside the dressing rooms were loading docks, closed off with chain link fencing, now covered with berserk Go-Go's fans climbing like monkeys and shouting and trying to break in. Boston cops did their best to keep order. It was threatening and exciting—but then, the crowd wasn't after me. The Go-Go's exited via another exit; we found some chowder, drove back to the motel, and caught a couple of hours' sleep before flying back to the West Coast.

Boston Calling

Douglas
Brian
Martin,
Santa Monica,
California

NOTHING WORTH HAVING COMES EASY

Opening for David Bowie on the Serious Moonlight Tour at Anaheim Stadium is something you could only wish for. So when it actually happened, I was extremely excited. I could hardly believe that this opportunity came our way. All I could think about was getting to meet him again, as I had met my hero once before when we were doing a show in New York City. We weren't even signed to a record deal yet and he came to see us. I hung out with him in the VIP room after our performance. I was in such awe I could barely converse with him. But I did. And so goes another first.

Back to Anaheim. Fortunately, my friend Gail Davis was working for Bowie at the time and I had been speaking to her about making this meeting happen. She came in, grabbed Kathy and myself, and ushered us into his dressing room. As always, such a gentleman, so elegant and personable. How lucky was I? When we finished playing, I stayed and watched his show. It was perfection. I know all of his material, and watching him perform those songs live from the side and the front of the stage was a breathtaking experience. This was the last show we did before we left to record our third album, *Talk Show*, in England. What a way to go!

Dare by the Human League was a breath of fresh air for me in the States. Sonically, the album was incredible. It was big and textural with gorgeous vocals driven by machine-like drums. Our live shows could be very unpredictable, which was a good thing for this band. That unpredictability resulted in an edginess I was hoping to bring to our third album. We wanted to find the right producer who could help us capture that aggressive, edgy feel and bring a richer, fuller sound overall. When Miles suggested the name Martin Rushent, the producer of *Dare*, I didn't need any persuading. I fully believed he would be the guy who would lead us to making a great record.

I couldn't wait to get to England to be influenced by my new surroundings. Different people, different music, and a different lifestyle—I looked forward to the experience. Martin's recording studio Genetic was located in Streatley, a sweet little sleepy town on the Thames. We blew in there already in bad-behavior mode, and I knew the road in front of us was going to be rough. The band was really starting to splinter. It seemed like everyone was using a lot of drugs, and we were not communicating in a real way. All conversations were very surface. No one really knew what the others were feeling and thinking, so when someone finally did speak up, it seemed to be coming from a place of anger. Not a comfortable situation. Despite ourselves, I did believe we'd pull it together. We were professionals and had been in the studio enough times to know how to make it all work.

The band stayed at the Swan Hotel. It was quite a picturesque scene, with houseboats dotting the river's edge. This was our little hideaway. Some of us had a fascination with graveyards back then. On tour, if time permitted, we would visit them. There was an old cemetery in the center of this town that Belinda and I would take walks through. It was beautiful, green, and peaceful. I remember the fresh, grassy smell. The headstones dated back to the 1500s and bore inscriptions with a person's name, their dates of birth and death, and then something unusual like "She fell asleep."

All bands operate differently. Some bring in twenty songs to be recorded and figure out what the single is going to be as they work on them. The Go-Go's, on the other hand, usually go into the studio knowing what the singles will be. "Head Over Heels" was

really strong, and we knew going in that it would be our first single. You could just tell. It had all the elements that make a hit song, beginning with the super-catchy piano intro and my four-on-the-floor kick drum. Then the guitar and bass jump in. With Martin at the helm guiding us, this song exploded. It sounded big and it sounded powerful. And Belinda's impressive vocals were so catchy. There were hooks all over the place. Guitar, bass, drums, piano—everything loaded with hooks. It's a great pop song. We still play it at just about every show.

"You Thought" was one of the songs that I had co-written with Kathy on the album. It is basically a relationship song where one person has tunnel vision on how things are going to work for the both of them. A flimsy faith that you are expected to follow without asking too many questions. Lyrically, most songs are part truth and part fiction. So goes this song. Before we left for England, the shell of the song had been established. I came up with a piano part that I would play over and over while I got the vocal melody where I wanted it to be. Kathy was a true collaborator and her input helped complete the song. Martin loved it when we showed it to him. He thought the end result was impressive.

We discussed the recording of the album *Dare* a lot. I told him how much I liked the song "Seconds." It evoked the drama of desperation. I wanted that same kind of tension and feel in "You Thought." The drumbeat was a solid 2/4 with a punchy compressed sound. Kathy came up with a memorable bass line that filled the bottom of the recording. The guitar was fluid and bold. Jane solidly played muted 1/8 notes until opening into the chorus, giving it a much-needed release from the tension created in the verse. Charlotte played the keyboard part succinctly. It was the impetus for the song. Then you add Belinda, the icing on the cake. She sounded strong and believable. And of course the always thoughtful backing vocals and beautiful harmonies.

Genetic Studios had all the latest gear available. One piece being the synclavier, which was a digital synthesizer. It was very impressive to have at the time. Not only was it the newest technology with regard to synthesizers, but it was also incredibly costly. I was a bit fearful of that sucker. I wanted to make sure I wasn't going to be made to feel obsolete by a drum machine. Whenever we were getting ready to record a song, I would ask Martin to give me the first shot. Fortunately, my timing is very good, so we wound up using my drum tracks most of the time. Also, we could combine the original drum tracks with sounds from the synclavier. The end result would be exactly what we wanted to hear. "You Thought" was a track that was recorded strictly with the synclavier, and that's what was needed to give it the right feel and sound. As you work on a song over a period of time, you can become very fond of certain parts you create. You can't let those parts become too precious, because sometimes you have to let go of them and agree to do what's best for the song.

This album was one of the most difficult recordings I had ever been a part of. I believed that sequestering the five of us out in the woods in this small town in England would bring us together. That didn't happen. It felt like everyone was still caught up in the drama that they had brought with them. It wasn't long before those issues erupted, and a couple of the girls even left the country. I distinctly remember Doug Martin, who designed the *Talk Show* album cover and directed the "Head Over Heels" and "Get Up and Go" videos, being flown in from LA to get a feel for the record and organize a photo shoot. We all took the train in to London, and when it was time to shoot, there were only four of us there. Someone was always missing. So when we got a call letting us know the Eurythmics were playing in Oxford (which was close to Streatley), we could not wait to take a break from our present situation. This was such a welcomed relief. Kathy already knew Dave Stewart so it made it way more comfortable seeing them perform and subsequently hanging out with them backstage after the show. Doug drove Belinda, Kathy, our tour manager Bruce Patron, and myself from Streatley to Oxford. The Eurythmics were a relatively new band at the time and they didn't have a lot of money to spend on a huge stage presentation. It was more just about watching Dave and Annie Lennox do their thing. What a great combination, they complemented each other beautifully on stage. The music was smart with intricate rhythms weaved by synths and guitars throughout their songs. Needless to say, I loved their show and was completely captivated. I couldn't wait to meet them afterwards. Dave and Annie

144

were sweet and unassuming. Dave's guitar playing was unique, rhythmic, and melodic. Annie's voice was so big and commanding that it didn't seem like it could come out of that little body. What a voice. I knew I would be a fan forever.

Going to see the Eurythmics play in the middle of watching my band coming apart gave me a moment to catch my breath and really think about everything. At that point, I made up my mind to stay focused, do my job, and let management and the record label deal with getting everyone back on track. I felt isolated during this recording process. I was very unhappy. We were under a lot of pressure to make a great record and outdo the sales of the *Vacation* album. The fact that we finished *Talk Show* is yet another testament to the band that we are.

Clown Family on Tour

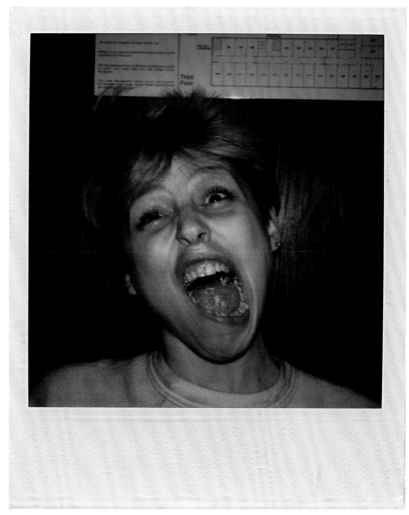

157

Aboard the Go-Go's Train

Dave Stewart,
Nashville,
Tennessee

I became close friends with Kathy Valentine around about the fall of 1983. Kathy was great fun to be around, and we often ended up crying laughing over what didn't really matter. I think we both were excited, surprised, and thankful that our music was actually allowing us to make a living, and that allowed unbridled creative craziness to ensue.

A vivid memory of the kind of craziness I mean was an outing via train from London's Paddington Station to Goring, about fifty miles west in Oxfordshire, to meet legend producer Martin Rushent, who was about to produce their album *Talk Show*.

I was excited to meet Martin, but I must say the train journey was a highlight of the outing, even beating the naked dancing in the woods in the dark (of which I didn't partake).

As the train began to pull out of Paddington Station, three of the Go-Go's, led by the forever bold and impish Belinda, followed by the courageous Gina and a rather shy Kathy, decided to run to the window, lift up their T-shirts, and expose their barely covered breasts to bowler-hatted commuters pulling in on the train alongside us, about ten inches from their window! The look of confusion, horror, and bewilderment from the opposite carriage is still imprinted on my brain, rather like a painting by Hieronymus Bosch, but the hysterical laughter that followed from the girls was infectious, and I must admit it was incredibly brazen and extremely funny. They were in full control, and they knew it, and one prank was followed very swiftly by another.

This time it was me who was horrified, as Gina screamed, "Corner Cleaners," and the same three merry pranksters leapt down on all fours and began to—at least to my eyes—lick the corners of the dirty carriage floor. (I was later to find out they only pretended to do this.) Nevertheless, the effect was pretty startling, and it took me a while to see the funny side, as I thought to myself that Kathy was great, but I wasn't sure about her hygienic qualities.

Anyway, we got to Genetic Studios, located somewhere deep in the woods, and I will stop there, as it became a bit of a blur, with the evening ending up at the Swan Hotel in Streatley, a quaint country town whose residents I'm sure had no idea what they were soon to be witnessing!

What's Important Here

Before we went on a major tour, everyone was scheduled to get a physical. It might have felt like a waste of time, but there was so much money involved even before we did our first show. Promoters needed to know the entire band was in good physical health before they spent a dime promoting the event. We all got our physicals, and only I got a call back with some unexpected news. Instead of getting a big thumbs-up, my primary physician, Dr. Roger Lerner, let me know I had a heart murmur.

This condition is not a death sentence; lots of people have it, and it mostly amounts to nothing. But no matter how reassuring Dr. Lerner was, it was hard to go against my nature as a worrier. Especially when I had to wear a monitoring device around my chest. That was supposed to last for one week, so when I got a call from the doctor's office at rehearsal only two days in, I immediately felt a little sick to my stomach. I dropped my sticks and walked to the phone. It was his assistant telling me to come into the office immediately. I got weak in the knees. I was so upset I started arguing with her, asking, "Why can't we just talk about it over the phone?" She repeated that the doctor wanted to speak with me in person and I needed to come in.

I went from being annoyed and angry to feeling light-headed and wobbly. All I could think was that something must be really wrong with me for them to insist I leave rehearsal and come right in. When I walked back into the room and told the girls, it got very quiet. It was hard for us to look at one another for fear of what our faces might reveal. They put their instruments down and insisted the five of us go together to hear the results. During the drive over to Cedars-Sinai hospital, no one spoke. We parked the car and walked up to Dr. Lerner's office. The nurse escorted me straight in. I sat down, and he slid a model of a heart across his desk toward me. *That* was when I fell apart. Because I was sobbing and shaking uncontrollably, the nurse burst in and gave me a shot of some kind of sedative.

Dr. Lerner was trying to explain that I had an atrial septal defect, a hole in my heart. I really didn't comprehend all that he was saying. I was so out of it from the news I just received and was barely able to hold my head up. Was this really happening to me? As unbelievable as it might have sounded, it was true. And lucky we found it when we did because the hole in my heart was the size of a golf ball. It would have been irreparable by the age of thirty, and in a couple of years, I would have died. I was twenty-seven at that time. It felt like I was stuck in a bad movie. The whole thing was absolutely surreal.

The band was brought in to see me. It was time to tell the girls. I couldn't say the words. Still in shock, I just lay on the exam table, sobbing. They asked questions, they held my hand, they cried, knowing it was serious. What a heavy scene. Prior to the big scary news, the band had not been in a good place. The making of the third album was very difficult. It felt like things were coming apart. Add into the mix lots of money, drugs, and booze. Things were getting out of control. We were not paying attention to one another, much less ourselves. So when something as serious and real as my heart surgery came up, it trumped all the petty bullshit that was happening at the time. I was about to face major surgery, an experience that I might not live through. This was very sobering news.

I couldn't call my mom and tell her. The words would not come out of my mouth. My mom was my best friend. My confidant. She and my father were my everything. I wanted them to be proud of me. Everything I was doing was to make them proud. I was afraid of the impact this news would have on their physical well-being when they found out that the baby of the family needed heart surgery.

Jane and I went back to my house. I asked her to be the one to tell my parents. I called, and my mom answered the phone. "Mom, Jane needs to tell you something. Are you standing up?"

"Yeah," she said.

"Well, sit down, Mom."

"What's wrong?"

"Just sit down." Then Jane got on the phone and told her. My mom and dad immediately packed everything in the Lincoln and began their cross-country drive from Baltimore to LA.

We postponed our 1984 summer tour a couple of months, and my surgery was scheduled for two weeks later. I made out a will, a disturbing, unpleasant thing to do at any age, much less in your twenties. The girls and I decided to have one big bash in case I didn't make it. We rented a Caddy and a Jag and went to one of our favorite spots in Palm Springs ready to hang out, relax, and be a band of five friends. Two Bunch Palms Resort offered all sorts of treatments—facials, massages, mud baths. I was thinking if I was going to die, I was going to pamper myself all the way to the grave. Out of all the party favors we brought with us, I was only allowed pot, Valium, and mushrooms. I was really high and we were all having fun and doing goofy stuff. It was all in typical Go-Go's fashion. That weekend will never be extinguished from my memory. In the history of the Go-Go's, I never felt closer to everyone in the band than I did for those couple of days.

This procedure was about to change the person that I was and the person that I would be from that point on. My mother and father walked beside me as I was wheeled to the room where the surgery would take place. I had a tattoo on my left wrist that I was forced to cover up with a Band-Aid every time I went home to Baltimore. My mom insisted that I do this as her mother, Regina Miskowski, always said, "Someone with a tattoo will not be allowed into the gates of heaven." I thought that I might die during this surgery, so I felt that I had to confess to my father that I had the devil's work on my wrist. This devil's work was just percussion notes. Anyway, those pre-op drugs were like a truth serum.

What had felt like such a big deal became nothing at that moment. I showed him the tattoo. My father just smiled and said, "Honey, I don't care."

The next thing I heard was my brother's voice. He sounded miles away, but actually he was standing right next to the bed trying to rouse me from this heavily medicated sleep. I was waking up in intensive care. Tubes were everywhere—chest, nose, mouth. Even though I couldn't speak, hearing my brother's voice completely comforted me. If I had died and this is what they call heaven, it was a good place to be. And if I was alive, that meant the surgery was successful and I would now have the time to live out my life.

So many cards, so many flowers. The nurses started taking them out of my room because they were using up too much oxygen. I asked that the flowers be shared with the other heart patients on the floor. During my time in the hospital, several friends visited me to make sure I was still alive. I don't remember everyone that came to see me besides my family, but a couple did stick out. For instance, Kathy coming in all cheery telling me that I was a fighter and I would get better sooner than I thought. She also bought me this cool, weird, off-brand vintage guitar. It had three pickups and a very unusual shape to the body. An extremely thoughtful thing for her to do because she knew my guitar collection and this would fit in perfectly. Then Belinda popped in. She was buzzing around the room like a wild woman asking me one question after the next about my surgery. All the time we were talking, I watched her do little bumps of blow (remember those little coke spoons that came with the small brown bottles). The next thing I knew she was asking me if I wanted to do a bump. I remember her and I laughing so hard. She always said and did things that made me laugh. Unfortunately, it was really painful for me to even breathe at that point as I still had tubes coming out of my neck, my stomach, and my nose. My surgery was less than a week old. Then I remember Jodie coming in to see me. She was still at Yale and on a break back in LA. She was terribly sweet to me, giving words of encouragement reinforcing the idea that it might take a little while to get better, but it was bound to happen because I was young and strong. New York City was where I initially met her with Rob Lowe. Jodie, Kathy, and myself had so much fun running from dinner to dinner, club to club. We were all living life large. I will never forget her kindness when I was weak as a kitten. We became dear friends.

I stayed in the hospital for one week and went home. Mom, Dad, and my brother stayed for a couple of months to help me recuperate. When I was finally able to walk again, the first thing I wanted to do was go into my studio, sit at my drum kit, and play. Let me tell you, it was quite painful. I knew it would take a while before my healing was complete. Even as I laid in bed trying to get better, my thoughts were very clear—get back on the drums and go out on tour with the band I love.

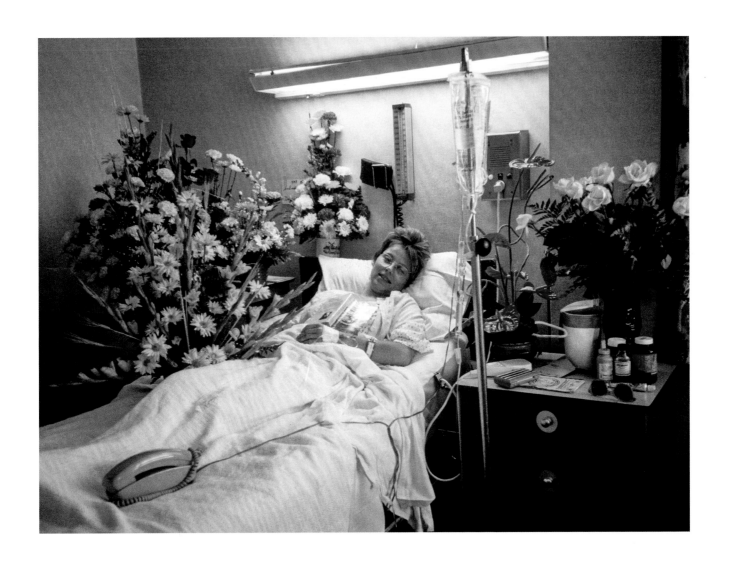

Too Much
is Never Enough

As a drummer, you need clear, precise concentration and muscle memory, and you need to know that you are one hundred percent capable of doing your job. The drummer is the foundation of every song. If you fuck it up, the rest of the band is in big trouble. Vocalists and guitarists can make mistakes and get away with it. Drummers can't. That's the way I've always approached my craft, so the thought of returning to rehearsals after surgery was weighing heavily on me. Since the age of thirteen, I had been playing drums, and my body was conditioned for that type of repetitive motion. Having your sternum sawed in half is an extremely difficult thing to go through. It's physically devastating, and what it takes to get yourself back is a traumatic experience. I was determined to get ready for the 1984 summer tour that was being set up for the band. Even though I was in a lot of pain, I made it a point to go into my studio, pick up the sticks, and play.

Every move I made frightened me because they had put my sternum back together with what really looked like little metal twisty ties. And I knew the bone was still healing. I was afraid my chest was going to crack open at any moment. At the same time, I definitely needed to get out of myself and out of the house. So when I heard John Mellencamp was playing at Universal Amphitheatre, I very gingerly got myself dressed and got in the car. I really enjoyed the show and wanted to go back and say hi. One of the first things John said to me when I saw him backstage that night was, "Hey, sister woman, you need to gain a little weight." He wasn't kidding. I weighed about ninety pounds. Although I was working on getting myself back together, I was still very weak. Soon after, management called to give me a Go-Go's update. They had scheduled a photo shoot for the cover of *Rolling Stone* with photographer Albert Watson. I was also informed that I had approximately two months to get myself together for that summer's Prime Time Tour. I had to always remember that management was there to guide my career and make me money. As much as that may have been true, it still felt a little harsh when I was told that I would have to be better by a certain date. I had to get my stamina back and gain weight, so I didn't look as sick as I was.

When we did summer tours, we always loved playing amphitheaters. We'd rather do three nights at the Greek than one night at the Forum, keeping in mind what the experience would be like for our fans. It seemed much nicer for them and for us to be playing under the stars on a beautiful summer night than being packed in an indoor arena. We began the tour at the Pine Knob Music Theatre right outside of Detroit on June 22, 1984. INXS was the opening act. What a perfect combination. I was already a fan of their album *Shabooh Shoobah*. They hadn't quite broken in the States yet. Their sound was new and fresh coming from Australia, which made it even better. We loved their accents, and they were all so good-looking. Each of us had a crush on someone in the band. Belinda and I would watch them from the side of the stage almost every night. Two of the songs I always waited for them to play were "The One Thing" and "Don't Change." Michael Hutchence was one of the best front men I had ever seen. He was a younger version of Mick Jagger. His performances had a very sexual tone. He was quite the showman.

Every night was something new with the boys and we were delighted to be on tour with them. I started to notice as the tour progressed that when they walked onstage, all the seats were full. People were there to see both bands. It reminded me of us a year earlier, when we were opening for the Police. One of the most important shows we have ever done happened the first week of that tour with INXS. It was Radio City Music Hall. INXS was really excited about playing there as well. Even in Australia they knew the importance of Radio City. Both bands had off the day before our show, so the party started at my friend's apartment and continued on to several clubs that evening. It didn't take long before Belinda and Michael were an item. At times, I felt a little like a third wheel. But I

loved Belinda, and Michael was such a personable, sweet guy. Easy to be around, and I suspect easy to fall in love with. We were staying at Le Parker Meridien, and it was only a couple of blocks away from the venue. Most of the time on tour you spend flying or driving. You rarely get to walk, so it was always nice when you could do something a little different. The next day we walked to Radio City to do our sound check early. I was dying to see the Rockettes' dressing room. I still have a vision from when I was a child of seeing the Rockettes on that stage. My parents took my brother and me several times to see the Christmas show there. It was beautiful, thrilling, AND live! That venue has such history. I added this experience to the list of things I will never forget.

Jane told us she was leaving the band. When I am faced with something that is upsetting, initially I get angry, then I get sad, and then I just try to push it out of my mind. We did the last show with her in San Antonio. You could feel a sadness. The air felt heavy. Stepping on that stage and sitting behind my drum kit was when I had the full realization that this might be the last time the five of us would play on the same stage together as the Go-Go's. We were doing our best to act happy and put on a good show. It was hard to look at Jane during that performance because I was already tearing up and didn't want to cry. I was thinking to myself, All these years together and this is it? The legacy that we created was ending in San Antonio? It would have been more appropriate if our last show was at the Hollywood Bowl, but you can't control what has already been put in motion.

Jane was always recognized for her contributions to this band as a songwriter, singer, and guitarist. And a big part of our sound is the mix of Belinda and Jane's voices together. I believe she certainly could have gotten a solo deal and stayed in the band. So I guess I never completely understood why she would leave the Go-Go's. Collectively, we wanted to keep things as they had always been. What a drag Jane left the band. Now, an original piece of the puzzle was missing.

We flew back to LA the day after our final show of the tour with only two and a half months to find a replacement. In January 1985, we were scheduled to play the first Rock in Rio festival. Our management put the word out that we were looking for a bass player. Kathy is, and always has been, a guitar player. The only reason she was the bassist in the band to begin with was because we needed one. So we thought, Let's let her do what she loves to do best and that's play guitar. It wasn't long after we were sitting in a rehearsal room looking through photographs, listening to tons of cassettes, and watching videotapes. It was going to be a difficult task to fill the shoes of someone in a band as big as ours at the height of our career. Eventually, we narrowed it down to four or five girls. However, that was when the going got tough. Sometimes two of us would make a choice and the other two girls would choose someone else. At one point it became clear that Paula Jean Brown was going to be the obvious choice. She was a good musician and a songwriter to boot. I really liked the fact that she was also a guitar player. That meant the choices in her bass playing would probably be more like Kathy's, which was a good sign to me.

Our first rehearsal with Paula Jean was in November. She came prepared and understood the dynamics of the band pretty quickly. One must remember she was walking into a mess. This was the height of our drug intake. Charlotte in particular seemed pretty out of control, and we all knew it but didn't know what to do about it. So I have to give Paula Jean extra props for being able to handle the situation in the graceful manner that she did. A good girl and a true professional. Things were moving really fast. We were also in the midst of contacting record producers to do the next record. We had a meeting with Keith Forsey. He had produced Billy Idol's *Rebel Yell*, and that was a hit record. There was so much to take in and absorb and not a lot of time to do it before Christmas break. The most important part was getting Paula comfortable and locked in with us as we got ready to play the biggest shows of our careers at the Rock in Rio festival.

It was apparent when we got to our hotel, the Rio Palace, that there was going to be a lot of partying going on. I am pretty sure that all the bands that were playing the festival had been booked there. Paula Jean was probably stunned by her new surroundings and finally experiencing what it was like being in a band of our stature. Photographers everywhere snapping shots of you, and there were journalists sticking microphones in your face asking questions. Then later on seeing rock stars up close, hanging out at the pool, having drinks, taking a swim, doing a line here and there. A lot of the biggest managers, agents, and bands in the world were hanging out together for a little over a week. This was really something to have been a part of.

The band was driven to a helicopter pad, where we were then flown to the festival area. Looking around as we were flying to the site, I noticed that the hills were all slums. In Brazil they're called favelas. The wealthier people lived in the flatlands, exactly the opposite of what I had been used to seeing living in Los Angeles. Hovering above the festival site and seeing 250,000 people in front of this huge stage was another incredible Go-Go's moment. We had never played in front of that many people before. From the perspective of the stage, the audience looked like ants. We were having a great time on stage feeding off the electricity of that tremendous crowd. Paula Jean played beautifully, looking confident and every bit a rock star. Then we stayed to watch Rod Stewart's performance. I had been a fan since the Small Faces and into *Every Picture Tells a Story* and onward. We hung out for a bit and decided to get together later for dinner. We met Rod and his band at Maxim's and had quite the elaborate meal. It was such a thrill to sit down and have dinner with Rod Stewart. Lots of champagne with several courses. That evening turned into an all-nighter. At seven a.m., I was still awake and ventured downstairs. I found Belinda all by herself, dressed in her baby-doll pajamas, smoking a cigarette and drinking margaritas lying by the poolside. Clearly, she had not slept either. What a sight! She looked like some fabulous movie star poolside having a cocktail in the afternoon. Except, it was seven a.m.

Our final show was fantastic. We were in fine form. Again, I stood on the side of the stage to watch the preceding bands. The B-52s have always been one of my favorites, and that night they had a special guest drummer and bass player, Chris Frantz and Tina Weymouth. The dynamic duo. When they played, it became a big party. Can you just picture 250,000 people dancing? Wow, what an incredible sight. Then Queen came on. Freddie Mercury stole the show. Recalling that moment I still get chills. The emotion behind his magnificent voice hit me in such a visceral way. He always had that effect on me. One of the greatest voices ever, certainly in rock history. And I was lucky enough to be witnessing all of this up close. The Pavarotti of rock 'n roll, captivating the crowd as they watched his every move and sang along with him. To see those two iconic bands play in front of that huge crowd was a night to remember.

The following evening I got a message from Kate Pierson. We were all meeting at a certain time in the lobby to go to Club Hippopotamus. It was pre-Carnival, and things were feeling electric. In the center of the club was a long runway where dancers performed wearing bikini-like garb and huge headdresses with plumes of feathers. The dancers with their beautifully full-shaped bodies were something to behold. The best part of the evening was when Kate got up on that runway and started dancing. Another incredible evening, and it was happening in Rio.

The morning we were leaving, I got up early to take a walk and give it all one last look. It was a very eventful trip. A lot jammed into a week and a half, including my meeting a very handsome guy who also happened to be the drummer in a hugely successful South American band. We spent most of the time I was there together. I knew I would miss him.

Sitting in first class with the Go-Go's was the band Whitesnake. I got to talking to the lead singer, David Coverdale. His sex-bomb persona made me always think of him as a jerk. During this flight, I completely changed my mind and realized he was a pretty swell guy. We talked for hours about the record business, his life, my life. He reminded me a lot of Gene Simmons, who I also like. I never spoke to him again, but what sticks out most during this short time we spent together was the last hour of the flight, when he got up to use the bathroom and came back perfectly coiffed, contact lenses in, moisturizer and a little bit of foundation on. When you are a lead singer, you have to know all the tricks of the trade. David got back, and I got up to use the restroom. On my way I noticed my elegant bandmate Belinda lying on the floor in the last row of first class, smoking a cigarette and having a drink. Yet another reason why I love being in the Go-Go's. We're all such kooks.

"Come on, Kate, join us," Jane called out from one of the backstage dressing rooms. When I walked into the room, I saw all five Go-Go's leaning over a long table—skirts up and their bare butts in the air, ready to receive the zing of their B_{12} shots from Dr. Feel Good.

It was year 2000, and we were on tour with the Go-Go's! I don't know why they needed energy, because they were the Go-Go's. Small but mighty, they were a collective bombshell of energy. In short skirts and combat boots, these women ripped up the stage like any rock 'n roll band should. During that tour, we rotated as opening and headlining acts, and they were always a hard band to follow.

We had done several other tours with them over the years, including Rock in Rio, a giant ten-day rock festival held in Rio de Janeiro in January 1985. The lineup was amazing and eclectic, including Queen, Ozzy Osbourne, Nina Hagen, and us: the B-52s and the Go-Go's. The Go-Go's were performing before us, and it was the first time I saw them live. Yes, they had the beat . . . and they played it with grit, enthusiasm, and glamour. Gina, unstoppable and reckless, powerfully driving the drums; Kathy slicing out waves of stingray guitar hooks; Charlotte rippling out surfy power chords; Paula Jean pumping up the bass velocity; and Belinda singing like a mermaid surfer girl. And they made you want to dance! As I watched them, I thought, What a fucking great band!

I can't remember who hosted us, but after we played, the B-52s and the Go-Go's were treated to one of those must-see shows at Club Hippopotamus with real Rio showgirls and samba. The MC said, "Let's get someone from the audience to come up here and do the samba!" He picked me. Little did he know I had just taken samba lessons in New York. When I got up to the stage, I really did some high-steppin'! We were all laughing, and the Go-Go's said, "Hey, let's go to a dance club!" An after-hours club was not usually our thing, but we thought, What the hell, we're with the Go-Go's, so let's go! While my memory was stemmed by tequila shots, I do remember they started playing punk music at the club and we all started dancing together. Of course they played "Rock Lobster" and "We Got the Beat" and the club went wild—everyone surrounding us while we danced the night away.

Emotionally, I feel such a connection to the Go-Go's. I have had more interaction with each member of that band than any other we've toured with. They had that super bond that forms when you're playing and touring together. Every woman in rock 'n roll gets tired of being asked about "women in rock." The really unique thing about the Go-Go's is their songs and their sound. They were songwriters and musicians first, and the hits just kept coming—songs that were full of heart, energy, soul, and a feel-good vibe. So it was never just about being women. It was that they delivered the raw energy of the time we were all living in. Their songs tell stories that glitter with girl-group gossip, strength, vulnerability, and sex appeal. Their melodies and harmonies . . . earworms for the ages.

Wild Times with the Go-Go's

Kate Pierson, Woodstock, New York

It's Later than You Think

Coming home after a wild tour and walking through my front door has always been the great leveler. It brings me right back down to earth. No handlers or big events. There aren't tens of thousands of people waiting to see you play. After the Rock in Rio shows, the band lost one another for a week or two, like we always did. Nothing compares to sleeping in your own bed in your own home, a feeling of security and comfort that doesn't happen anywhere else. You come to miss all the familiar places. Taking a walk around your neighborhood. Going to restaurants you love. Seeing your friends. These things matter.

By the time we got back to Los Angeles, Charlotte was deep in her addiction. We really feared for her life. Our newest member, Paula Jean, found a rehab in Pasadena for her to enter. We gave our blessings. This was something that was way overdue. None of us were in a good place. We had all taken drugs, just not to the degree that Charlotte had. I remember the doctor saying she would have only lived a few more months at the rate she was going. Kathy and I visited her in rehab a couple times a week. We would smoke pot before we got there because we were so nervous and had no idea what to expect. Walking into that environment was shocking. Seeing addicts in various stages of getting off their particular drug of choice. It was scary. I could only imagine what Charlotte must have been going through in the time she spent there alone. It was different and new every time we saw her. Sometimes she would blame us for her situation, and other times she was grateful that Kathy and I were there. I now understand this behavior after being in several rehabs myself. Back then, I didn't.

Initially, we all started out taking drugs because they were fun, but it ends up getting ugly when it becomes a habit. Being in the music business, I have known lots of people who have been in rehab. And most wind up going back many times before they kick their addiction. Charlotte was in rehab only once and has been sober ever since. That is a little shy of a miracle, as far as I'm concerned. We could see her getting better over her twenty-eight-day stay. When she was released, we were so relieved to get her back. I was hoping that this would help us connect in a way we never had before. And we were now in the process of putting the necessary pieces together to do our next record.

In between these major events in all our lives, I did have some time to relax. I was lying on the couch when the phone rang. It was Belinda: "Are you doing anything this evening?" She wanted to know if I was interested in going to the Playboy Mansion with her and Morgan. (He was not yet her husband, but within a year they'd be married.) I didn't want to miss this trip. We met and drove to the Playboy Mansion off Sunset. It was everything I imagined and then some. The place truly was surreal. When we pulled up, a valet took our car and we were escorted into the mansion. The grounds were palatial. We walked around, taking it all in as we giggled and were served champagne. The world that Hugh Hefner dreamed of as a young man in Chicago had now become his reality in Los Angeles. His imagination was in full swing, surrounding him on the estate. Exotic animals all over the grounds, Playboy Bunnies sauntering around, and the who's who of Hollywood visiting every night. The areas around the grounds of the mansion had different names. There was an underground cave called "the grotto." It was steamy and dimly lit. This is where we happened upon two people in the pool having sex. They seemed not to notice us. We, on the other hand, were slightly mortified. By this time, Belinda and I were pretty high and laughing at everyone and everything. We just kept wandering around and eventually found Morgan talking to Hef. There he was in his smoking jacket, puffing on his ever-present pipe, with a girl on each arm. He was very

charming, quite the gentleman. The three of us had so much fun that night, but on my drive home, I thought that living that life day in and day out might make you a little crazy. Just spending one night there seemed like I was going into some altered reality. It was fun for a minute.

We were writing and demoing songs for the next record, but things were different this time around. Jane had quit, Charlotte had been in rehab, and we had a new member in the band. Kathy was playing guitar instead of bass. Things were kind of mixed up, and we were trying to organize everything with all the changes that had just taken place. I remember we were arguing a lot. Paula Jean was shocked at the way we treated one another. What we needed then more than anything else was a long-deserved rest. Taking a year off would have been a good idea. We were run-down and tired out. It really felt like the people we had chosen to guide us were looking strictly at the bottom line. The bottom line was generating enough money to fill everyone's pockets. We were now at a tipping point and desperately needed someone to take the reins, to tell us to stop and give it a break. In April, our *Talk Show* album went gold, but that didn't seem to matter because we were all mired in our own little dramas. This was keeping us from making smart, thoughtful decisions.

On May 3, 1984, I wrote in my journal, "I hate this band. I left rehearsal." We had everything, and we were blowing it. Still, we continued rehearsing every day. But on May 10, instead of going to rehearsal we all went to meet up for lunch at our manager's office. Kathy and I arrived together. Charlotte and Belinda were already there. I knew something really fucked up was about to happen because when we walked into the room there was complete silence. Then came the big news: Charlotte and Belinda were breaking up the band. It took the breath out of me. I felt like I had been punched in the stomach. All along I believed we were working hard, trying to keep things together. Little did I know, there was a lot going on that did not involve Kathy or myself. And that's how it went down. It felt like such a betrayal. As a team, we worked so hard to create something that we only dreamed of, and now it was over. It was hard to believe two people whom I considered family were doing this. I had no say-so in the matter and it broke my heart.

Kathy and I were furious leaving our manager's office. We stood outside and talked for a while before getting in our cars. As furious as I was, the anger was more surface. I was deeply wounded. When things like this happen, I call my mom. I did exactly that as soon as I got home. She was aware I had been unhappy with the band for quite a while, but I always held the belief we could work it out. After speaking with her, I did feel a little better. She gave me back faith in myself, enforcing the idea that ultimately things would be okay because I was talented and a hard worker. Within a couple of hours, the press started calling, wanting to talk about the breakup. It seemed glaringly obvious to me that the decision to break up was not made at that meeting. How crazy is it that a band that had come so far still did not have the ability to communicate with one another? And where in the hell was the management that was supposed to never allow something like this to go down?

I want to address the importance of songwriting in this band and whether the revenue generated by it should have been split equally among the five of us. When you write a song you want as many people as possible to be able to hear it. Basically you need a platform to launch it from. The band, the Go-Go's, was our platform. Without it, we stood an extremely slim chance of large numbers of people ever hearing anything we had written. We were pretty decent musicians whose contributions really made the sound that was the Go-Go's. Belinda, Charlotte, Jane, Kathy, and myself put our stamp on each song by the parts we individually came up with. I couldn't have imagined any of our songs becoming what they ultimately became without that stamp. Example: "We Got the Beat" without that drum beat? The band needs the songs and the songs need the band. It's a fifty-fifty thing. That is why I have always believed as far as money went it should have been split equally. It was the five of us that worked nonstop to push the Go-Go's to rock stardom and into a whole other income category.

In the months that followed, Kathy and I spent a lot of time working on a new band. Finding the right lead singer was difficult. You really have to have what it takes to front a band. A big personality, an original look that is true to you, the charisma that makes people want to watch your every move onstage, and the most important ingredient: talent. The audience has to believe that the words flowing from your mouth are coming from your soul. We tried for quite a while to find the right lead singer. Unfortunately, things never seemed to gel. Artistically, Kathy and I weren't on the same page, so we decided to give it a break. Meanwhile, Belinda had a record deal and was already working on her new album with Charlotte. "Mad About You" was released as the first single. This was one of the songs we were working on for the Go-Go's next record. This hit me pretty hard, but it also helped me to get hyper-focused to find a new partner in crime. I found Vance DeGeneres.

Vance was a bass player and a songwriter from New Orleans. He was a handsome guy with a fantastic personality. Everything clicked with him and me. We meshed beautifully and were definitely the right combo for the foundation of House of Schock. Vance and I began writing songs as we simultaneously started looking for other players to complete the lineup. Once all the pieces were in place, we started rehearsing in my studio. It became apparent as things progressed that I should be the singer. I just wanted to write and play drums. But since we had been rehearsing with me singing, it was a comfortable transition and very satisfying for me to be able to sing the songs I had written. For the first time no one was interpreting them. It was coming straight from the source, and that was a powerful feeling.

I had a long relationship with Miles Copeland and asked him if he was interested in managing House of Schock. He listened, liked what he heard, and became our manager. We began rehearsing at his house in the Hollywood Hills. For several months, we worked on writing songs, then arranging them, and doing whatever else it took to make this new band happen. Being a lead singer was harder than I had imagined. To capture the audience's attention and keep it over the course of an hour or an hour and a half is no easy task. I realized I never gave Belinda as much credit as she deserved.

January 7, 1987, was our premiere performance at the Roxy. Invitations were sent out to one and all at record labels. The show was sold out. Walking onstage and knowing it's a full house puts you in the perfect frame of mind. I was hoping at least to get some label interest, so I couldn't believe after doing that one show, we were offered a record deal. This made me think of my journey from drummer to songwriter to singer and now to my first solo deal. A few months later, the ink was dry on the contract and House of Schock had signed with Capitol Records. I was so unsure about my future after the Go-Go's broke up, and this reassured me that I was truly capable of anything I tried to do with regard to music. When I thought of Belinda and Charlotte, I vacillated back and forth between anger and sadness. This record deal allowed me to drop the upset I felt when I thought about them. I couldn't wait to start my record and see what the future held for me as a solo artist.

Vance DeGeneres, Los Angeles, California

Most people know me from either music or comedy. I've been lucky enough to have successful careers in both fields. If you only knew me from House of Schock, or one of my other bands, you'd probably be surprised to learn that I was the original Mr. Hands in *The Mr. Bill Show* from *Saturday Night Live*, and I was one of Jon Stewart's original correspondents on *The Daily Show with Jon Stewart*, among many other comedy gigs.

This is my way of saying I love music and I love comedy. And I enjoy combining the two whenever possible. So, what nobody knows about HOS: We could've done an album of comedy songs.

We rehearsed at the house of our manager, Miles Copeland. He lived in the Hollywood Hills in a cool old mansion that had a guesthouse where we and his other band, the Police, rehearsed. To get onto the property, you had to ring the gate bell, which also alerted Glub and Pasha, a couple of two-hundred-pound mastiffs. You'd be buzzed in and immediately see the two beasts running full speed toward you. They just wanted to say hello, but I don't think Gina appreciated their warm welcome.

We were diligent about rehearsing and worked hard on getting our material ready to play live and to record in the studio. But in between our regular songs, sometimes we'd mess around and come up with some comedy songs as well. Everyone knows that Gina is a great drummer, but I don't think people know how funny she is.

For example, there was our polka version of Black Sabbath's "Iron Man." Then there was a country song we wrote called "Two Boots Make a Pair" that Gina and I sang as a duet. Some lyrics: "You're a miserable woman. And you're a miserable man. We get together and . . . two boots make a pair." Rhyme? We don't need no stinking rhyme. Gina and I could've been the Porter Wagoner and Dolly Parton of the eighties.

We did a surreal version of the Everly Brothers' "Wake Up Little Susie." Imagine it slowed down, with a minor chord added to sound extra creepy, me basically talking the lyrics, and Gina with a sleepy "I'm awake" at the end of every verse. Then there was the song we wrote for our manager, "The Theme from Miles." It was a funny/cool instrumental that sounded like the Ventures meet the Cramps.

Maybe my favorite was one when Gina and I did our best Porter and Dolly over a bizarre sort of samba beat, with a cheesy synthesizer part, called "Ain't Not Got You." Lyrics: "I ain't too smart, I ain't too funny, I ain't got looks, and I ain't got money." Then Gina and I would trade off on "But I ain't not got you." A gem of a love song.

I really wish we had put them out as an EP. Our label, Capitol, might not have been very happy if we had done that, but I think it would've been a big hit on *The Dr. Demento Show*.

Gina, Steven, Chrissy, and Jim all had good senses of humor, and we had some of our best times, crying with laughter as we wrote and rehearsed these comedy songs that would never see the light of day outside of our rehearsal studio. You might ask: Why would you waste your time? Why wouldn't you just rehearse your regular material? Well, first of all, you should mind your own business, and secondly, when bands rehearse too much, they can get burned out and the material starts to feel stale. Injecting some laughs into rehearsals helps to keep things light and fresh.

I think I laughed as much during those House of Schock rehearsals as I did during my time on *The Daily Show* or any other comedy show I did after HOS. And that atmosphere translated into the recording studio when we recorded our debut album for Capitol. Good times.

HOUSE OF SCHOCK

Let's Work Together

I like to work with other people. The fact that I have always been in a band exemplifies that. When I am part of something bigger than myself, I tend to learn more, which elevates my craft. I am a much better songwriter when I have a partner. Vance understood me and what my vision was for this band. Everybody else we brought in was a real asset, and we all complemented one another.

Tom Whalley was the head of A&R at Capitol and also the guy who signed us. We had already written most of the songs for the album, and it was time for us to sit down and figure out who we were going to get to produce the record. We decided to bring in my old buddy Richard Gottehrer, because he was a song man. He flew to Los Angeles, and we soon got together at a rehearsal room to get the songs into shape; we were eager to start recording. It was decided that we would do the record in the basement studios of the Capitol Records Building. That's the place where the Beatles held their press conference when they first arrived in Los Angeles. I was really excited to be recording my first solo record in those historic studios. We had already worked out any problem areas in the songs, and the arrangements were pretty much done. The time we spent working with Richard was always a pleasure and very productive. He really is a great producer. I feel lucky to have been able to work with him the several times that I have.

We finished the record, and Richard flew back to New York. Tom Whalley and I decided that we wanted to record a couple of more songs and do a couple of remixes. We knew that "Middle of Nowhere" would be the single, so more attention would be required. Chas Sandford was brought in to do the job. He was a producer and a songwriter known at the time for the John Waite hit "I Ain't Missing You." We recorded two new songs and worked on "Middle of Nowhere." After several weeks of concerted efforts, the record was radio ready. Chas was very talented and easy to work with. The album was completed, and next we concentrated on making the video for the single, bringing in Mary Lambert to direct. She had done several videos for the Go-Go's, so I knew her work ethic. She could take a song and expand on it in a visual sense. We had fantastic results working with Mary, which was no surprise. I loved the record, and I loved the video. It was time for House of Schock to go out and do some shows.

What happened next took us all by surpise. We were in touring mode when we got the word that a regime change happened at the label. We had a decision to make: Should we stay and hope the new team would support us, or should we look for another record company? Staying under those circumstances is typically very risky, so we chose to leave. It seemed all our efforts didn't amount to what we had hoped for, and it wasn't long afterward that Vance and I decided to part ways. I felt like I needed a break, so I went to New York City, which has always been my second home. There's no place on earth like it, and when House of Schock ended, I went back there to regroup and contemplate my next move. I decided to give up the idea of being in a band and began focusing on becoming a full-time songwriter. Eventually, I got a publishing deal with MCA, and that kept me happy for quite a while. I also had a great apartment overlooking the East River and would often travel to Baltimore via Amtrak to see my parents. On the many train rides back and forth was where I would do my best uninterrupted thinking. I would recount my life in little snapshots and then full screen. The full screen always included the Go-Go's. No matter where I went or what I did, they always loomed large in my psyche. We all had followed our solo endeavors, but there is something to be said about how the Go-Go's came together. All of us coming from different places, different backgrounds, and finding one another in Hollywood. I believe our destinies were set to converge at that particular

time in our lives. It's incredible how things happen. And whatever the reasons may be, all the parts fit perfectly for the Go-Go's.

The band had been broken up for five years. It was now 1990. We found out Jane Fonda was trying to contact the band. That came by way of Danny Goldberg, the head of Gold Mountain Management and also Belinda's rep. She wanted to talk with us about doing a show to raise money for the California Environmental Protection Initiative. Everyone was busy with their solo careers, so getting the five of us all in one room wasn't going to be that easy. However, with the Go-Go's being environmental activists, and Jane Fonda being Jane Fonda, how could we say no? That started the ball rolling. We had several meetings and dinners with her to discuss things. We decided to do a show at Universal and were more than happy to donate all the proceeds to this green initiative. The night before the event, we played our first concert with our Jane since she had quit the band. We wanted it to be a surprise show, so we were billed as KLAMM on the marquee (use your imagination for this one). Don't ask me where we come up with this goofy stuff, but we think it's funny and always wonder if anyone else ever gets our humor. It felt so good to be playing back at the Whisky, just like old times.

I am sure Jane Fonda has the ability to get anyone to work with her in any capacity. You can only imagine how blown away we were when she chose us to work on a cause that was dear to our hearts. I didn't have a lot of female role models growing up, but I must say she was one of them. Outspoken and beautiful—that struck a chord in me. Being a woman back in the sixties may have been a disadvantage when it came to politics, but it wasn't for her. She was a feminist and a sex symbol who fought for civil rights and so much more. A deeply passionate woman, and any cause that she was involved in you knew was worth fighting for. We met several times at her house, and something that stayed with me were the many photographs of her family. It was obvious that family was important to her. She was a good listener. That says a lot about someone.

The band was hanging out a lot more. We set up dinners and started calling one another to discuss our future. Within a couple of months, we actually began writing new material. Then we planned a fall tour and all that went with it. That meant lots of rehearsing and doing our first new video since 1984. We had talked for years about recording "Cool Jerk" as a one-off single. It was a favorite of ours, and the audience always reacted strongly when we played it. The timing was perfect to do a dance remix. David Z, a producer who worked with Prince at Paisley Park, was the right guy. David was also a drummer, so he and I spoke the same language. I flew to Minnesota to work on the drum tracks first. Paisley Park was a huge complex that housed everything Prince. When I walked in and looked around, I realized he had no reason to ever leave. There were people making his clothes, there were people making his food, and the studios were open for whenever he decided to work. A musician's dream. It took three days to record the drum tracks. Then David and I flew to LA to begin recording with the rest of the band. Management was busy setting up our fall schedule. We had a new song, a new video, and a performance set for November 9 on *Letterman*. We were on track, and it felt good. The family was back together.

Over the next decade, we stayed busy with our own projects and the Go-Go's continued touring regularly. We released *Return to the Valley of the Go-Go's* in 1994. It consisted of three new studio songs and thirty-three different versions of songs from our catalog. That included some live, some acoustic, and actual cassette tapes from rehearsals. This compilation brought back a lot of memories, because at least five of the songs were written in '78 and '79 but never put on an album. Several years had passed while we continued to tour. During that period of time, we started talking about making a new record. Everyone had been writing separately and together, so there was lots of material to choose from. We wound up signing with Beyond Management. The band discussed several producers and decided on Sean Slade and Paul Kolderie, who had produced the Hole album *Live Through This*. Being multi-instrumentalists and songwriters, they knew from top to bottom the process of writing a song, arranging it, and producing it.

God Bless the Go-Go's is full of great songs and definitely one of my favorites. "Throw Me a Curve" and "Sonic Superslide" were songs that had been written by the band at my studio. When all of us were in one room working on the same song, it could become a little tense, because everyone winds up having several opinions about the same thing. So how did we figure out which was the right choice? Ultimately, we always did. "Automatic Rainy Day" was a song that I had written for my latest band, K5. I showed it to the girls, and they really liked it. Jane came in, changed a couple of the lyrics, and the song was done.

205

206

Sean and Paul captured a full chunky sound from the guitars with the edginess of a live show. The guys were also very complimentary of my playing, thereby giving me the confidence to knock one song out after the next. They did a great job recording the drums. I was very happy with the end result. They also did a great job recording the whole band, for that matter. Kathy's bass was rich and precise. Belinda's vocals sounded better than ever.

I wonder if this will be the last album we ever do. There have been so many times over the past forty years that we wanted to call it quits, but something happens and we can't walk away. However, if this is the last album, I am very proud of it. The songs are really good and the production is truest to the sound we always wanted. But I really hope it's not. My favorite things are recording and going on tour. I love working with this band despite the ups and downs. All of my solo accomplishments may never have happened if it wasn't for the Go-Go's. This band has afforded me so much in life. It's a gift. I can't forget it and never will deny it.

The GO-GO'S are Never Over

We all requested that our star on Hollywood Boulevard be right in front of the old Pussycat porn theater. In that crummy basement is where we spent a lot of time with our friends, and they were all in bands. We'd hang out, get high, and share everything, because nobody had any money. Usually, the people who had jobs would buy the beer and then share it with everyone. So much started at that very spot. When we were rehearsing at the Masque, some nights we'd get pretty loaded and venture out of that stink pit (I say that affectionately). We'd check out all the freaks, but mostly we looked to see who had a star on the boulevard. I always thought that getting a star was the ultimate achievement for anyone. Think about the millions of people who come from all over the world just to experience walking down Hollywood Boulevard, knowing that the star they are standing in front of was once where someone they may have idolized stood. People are deeply moved by music and film, and I doubt that will ever change.

The Roosevelt Hotel was the scene where we were getting prepped for the Walk of Fame event, reminiscing and being silly as always. Telling the same jokes that only we laugh at and making fun of one another's outfit malfunctions. I gotta say, we really do have fun when we're together. When we got to the location on Hollywood Boulevard, it was rock star time, with everyone yelling our names. The fans gave us a warm welcome; their clapping and carrying on made the event feel like it was a mini Go-Go's show. Many of my dear old friends showed up at the ceremony. When I look at the photos from that day, I get a little choked up because it is a moment in music history that is strictly ours.

And getting that star on Hollywood Boulevard reinforced the fact that we had made it. This achievement is in my top five. We never thought about gender, but certainly the industry did. Our goal was to make it in the record business. To show people we had something to say and that hard work really does count. We were fighters, and with the five of us together that's one mighty force.

Los Angeles is still home base for the band even though we are scattered all over the globe. So before we begin a tour, I always have to go back there. I need to rehearse on my own for at least two weeks. Rehearsal is about fine-tuning and getting physically conditioned before you hit the road. It takes time to put together a good set. We need to sit down and go over our songs and make sure we are picking ones that the fans want to hear. Then we need to practice each one, getting them tight and making sure that one song flows into the next. As I like to say (ad nauseam), "It never hurts to practice. It only makes you better." That's always worked for me, and I continue to follow that axiom. We don't sound dated in any way. We sound current, and I attribute that to keeping our punk roots intact.

When we're playing on stage together, there is a chemistry happening that cannot be repeated. The Go-Go's live are a hard act to follow. No pyrotechnics, choreographed moves, or stage props. Although sometimes, if we have a real day off you might find us at a thrift store picking out the undesirables. On one tour we were shopping at a thrift store on Long Island and found several hideous paintings. A hand with six fingers playing piano was my favorite. We couldn't wait to get to sound check and figure out where we were going to place these beauties on the stage, as they were there strictly for our amusement. A Go-Go's crowd doesn't need any distractions. When we play, it's about watching the band and celebrating music. With the first drumbeat, the audience is already on their feet. They wind up dancing practically the entire evening. The energy flows from the audience to the band. The adrenaline is pumping so hard it takes me half of the show to calm down and relax into playing. It's like being swept up in a tornado and then dropped in the middle of a party.

The five of us have worked so hard to make the brand as valuable as it has become and it feels really good to say that the money issues have been cleared up in the last

several decades. No one needs to feel as though their contribution is not as valuable as the other. We each contribute something that doesn't happen when we do it elsewhere. This is gold. And this is what makes it uniquely Go-Go's.

Our band has been through a lot. Speaking strictly for myself, I am happy to be alive and able to put this book together. The drugs. The scary plane rides. The heart surgery. Somebody up there likes me. As for the rest of the girls, they would probably say the same thing minus the heart surgery. I am very grateful to have them in my life. We've grown up together. There have been marriages, divorces, and some of us have children. No relationship is perfect, and ours is not the exception. One day I am so fed up with one of the girls that I never want to speak to them again. Give me a week or two and all is forgiven. There is a true, deep connection here. We are family. That will never go away. Our accomplishments will remain. The legacy of this band will live on.

The Go-Go's are never over.

216

I Want My Head Over Heels

Martha Quinn,
San Francisco,
California

When the news about the Go-Go's *Head Over Heels* Broadway show first started to hit the press, all my MTV compadres were super jazzed. Joining the esteemed ranks of shows like *Beatlemania* and ABBA's *Mamma Mia!*, *Head Over Heels* was bringing the Go-Go's to Broadway! For us, with MTV and the Go-Go's being so intertwined in the eighties, it almost seemed like our video music channel was getting a nod in the process.

There was a current-day connection to *Head Over Heels* for me as well. My all-eighties music radio station (iHeart 80s @ 103.7) is located in San Francisco, so when the play was opening at the Curran Theater in the Bay, we were all over it. We even took an ad out on the back cover of the *Playbill*, shouting out "Martha's Mixtape" and I am not gonna lie: I was thrilled! On the big night, Kathy Valentine, Jane Wiedlin, and Charlotte Caffey were in attendance, my station had excited winners in the audience, I was there with my executive producer Christie James. I can tell you the atmosphere in the theater was buzzing. Everybody was thrilled to see the band they'd loved since the eighties be the subject of a grand theatrical presentation. We'd already heard it was an Elizabethan setting, which everyone couldn't wait to see. When the curtain went up, from the balcony to the orchestra, the Curran went bonkers. I was on cloud nine seeing the Go-Go's music recognized in the legitimate setting of Broadway. From my seat I could see the excitement in Kathy's, Jane's, and Charlotte's faces. I spent half the night watching the show, half the night watching them. It was a beautiful experience. It was kind of like when you see your child get an award and you feel so proud. The night was a massive party. Yay for the Go-Go's, yay for all of us! We're still here, we're still rocking, and we still love each other. Let's raise a toast!

One of the great aspects of MTV was how it brought a glimpse of an outside world to many who may not have fit in with the vibe of their town. Kids on the fringe were given a lifeline when they saw that a tribe for them did exist in the world! The Go-Go's were part of that accomplishment, with their upbeat yet gritty music as well as their self-styled punky, vintage fashion. Furthermore, the outfits they wore were ones we could all put together from shopping at our local secondhand store, which created a sense that everyone was invited to the party. It all came full circle the night *Head Over Heels* premiered at the Curran. The party was still going!

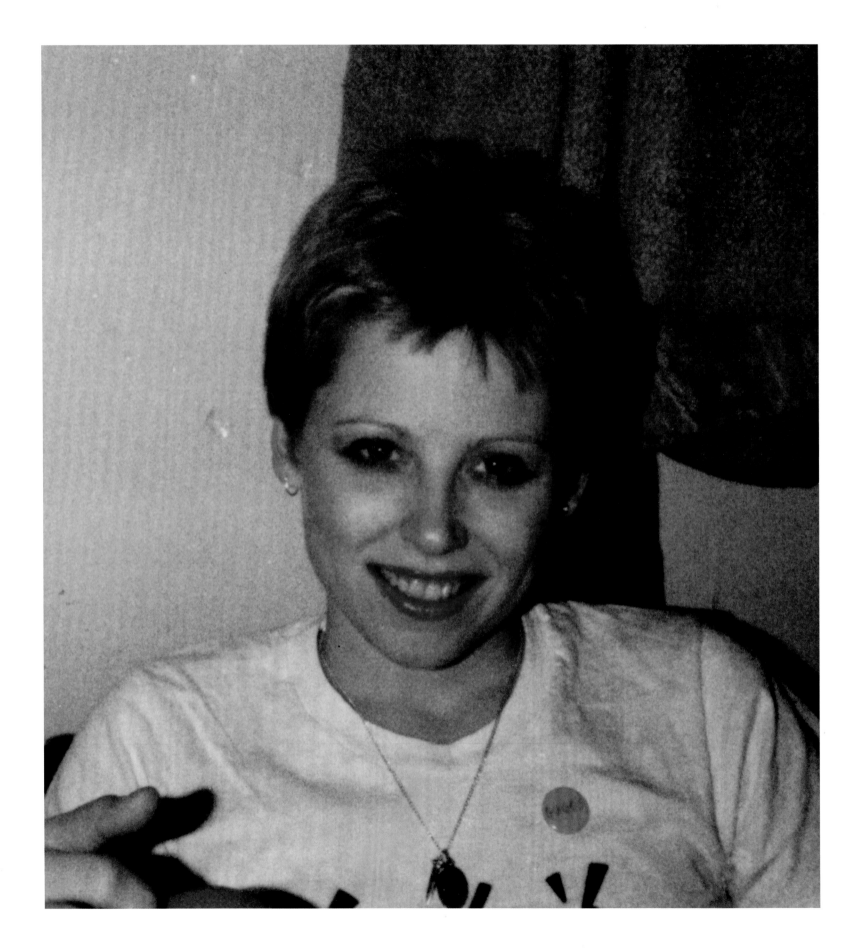

Acknowledgments

This book has been at the top of my wish list for quite a long time. I finally made it happen and I am super happy with the end result. I hope everyone loves it as much as I do. A labor of love can be a gift.

Ultimately, the majority of my life is replayed in these pages, and I wasn't alone. Let me start with the most important, my parents and my brother, who have influenced me in innumerable ways . . . and certainly all for the better. Oh, how I love them. Also, my high school friends, Rosie and Babs. I met Rosie my first day at Catholic High. We became immediate best friends and we still are. Rosie, I love you dearly. I got to be better friends with Babs my senior year. We were like-minded girls. Driving across the country together was a trip full of hope and uncertainty. Babs, we've been through a lot together. I still love you.

This band has been on such a long journey. Some really great times and some really rough times. We have grown up together and helped shape each other's lives. As I have said many times, we are family. Don't mess with the best! By the way, Kathy, thank you for writing the glowing foreword. Babe, Jane, and Charlotte, so overjoyed you gals could each write a story to place in the pages of my book.

Steve Martin, Doug Martin, and Relah Eckstein were the first people I met when I arrived in Los Angeles in the fall of 1978. We became friends. It's 2021 and they are still very dear to me. They contributed to this book. Doug, you did a fantastic job of art design. Clean, clear, and beautiful. Steve, thank you for all the time on the phone helping me remember so much about the early part of my life in Los Angeles. And dear Relah, who always had a camera with her when we were hanging out, thank you for the photos in this book, which are so very important in telling the Go-Go's story. I adore you.

Ginger Canzoneri, you allowed us to be who we were and so smart in guiding us with love, intelligence, and foresight. You never backed down and never took no for an answer. I can't thank you enough. Nice cover shot, baby!

Thank you, Frank Weimann and the whole Folio Literary Management. Frank, you are the coolest. No bullshit, just the straight-up info. So happy you're on my team. Thanks Scott Sigman, you're the best. AND a big thank you to my book publisher, Black Dog & Leventhal. What a process! I couldn't be happier with the end product. Thanks to one and all.

Visual Presentation, fantastic job! Jeanne Hangauer and Taina Kissinger, you girls knocked it out of the park. Cheers!

DW Drums, Paiste Cymbals, ProMark Sticks, and Evans Drumheads. You guys are tops!

Susan Tenby, you have always had my back. You are very dear to me. Much love, always.

Wendell Goodman, I love your guts. I am so grateful you are in my life.

Divina Infusino, thank you for all your great advice, my friend.

All the story and art contributors, thank you. I am so fortunate.

My little Penny, who gives me her unconditional love every day.

Dad, I am so happy you are still with me. ♥ ♥

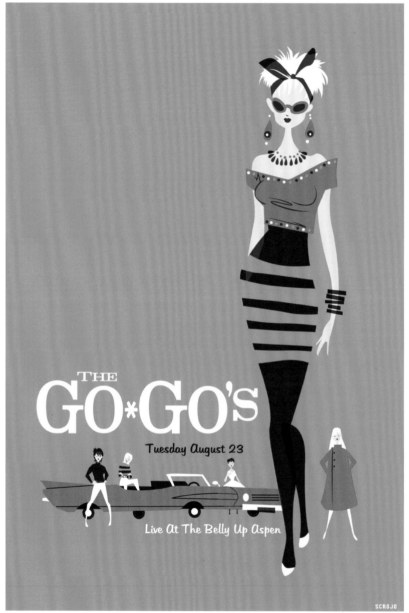

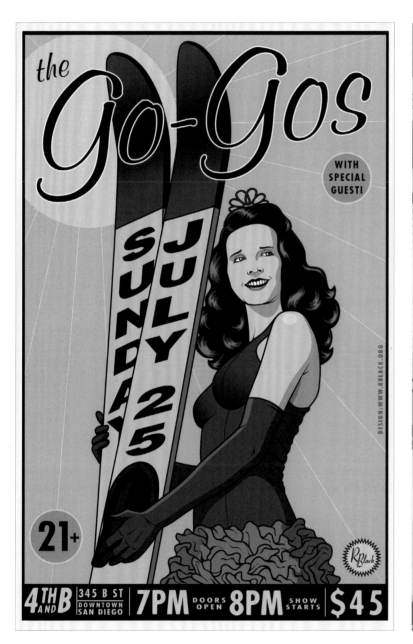

Photo Captions

Page ii: Self-portrait taken on tour in Japan in 1982.

Pages iv–v: (Left) Ready for my close-up, Mr. DeMille. (Right) Easter Sunday.

Pages vi–vii: (Left) Another Easter Sunday, another year. (Right) This is my Sacred Heart of Mary yearbook photo. My mother used to cut my hair.

Page viii: Japan in 1982.

Page x: Kathy, beam me up, Scotty.

Pages xii–xiii: (Left) Me, front row center, 3rd grade. Look at that face! (Right) My '70s rock 'n roll bedroom.

Page xiv: (Left) My 1957 WFL. That's a Ludwig snare drum, folks! (Right) The ticket stub from my first concert.

Page xvi: This is the first drum kit and cymbals I ever bought. The drums are a Japanese brand called Lido Supreme.

Page 3: My second drum kit: a Slingerland set from the 1970s with red, white, and blue sparkles. Check out the hair and headphones.

Page 5: Scratch 'n Sniff rehearsing in Charles Freeman's basement sometime around 1976.

Pages 6–7: Backstage photos at the Marble Bar in 1977. From left to right, that's George Kondylas, Danny Brown, yours truly, and Charles Freeman. In the forefront is our manager Chris Mason, who was also the hair stylist for all John Waters's films during that period of time.

Page 8: A 1978 flyer for an Edie and the Eggs show at the Nuart Theatre on Santa Monica Boulevard in Los Angeles.

Page 11: Onstage with Edie and the Eggs at the Nuart Theatre.

Pages 12–13: (Left) I keep everything. This is a matchbook from the Edie and the Eggs show at Max's Kansas City and some show notes from around the same time. (Right) John and Edie, Mudd Club, 1981.

Pages 14–15: (Left) At the Fiorucci party in Beverly Hills. (Right) Found at a thrift store in Baltimore.

Page 16: Photos taken on the drive from Baltimore to Los Angeles.

Page 19: Presenting my father's truck: a Ford Explorer.

Page 20: Big mouth.

Pages 23 and 24: Photos of me at the Beverly Glen party.

Pages 26–27: (Left) Me, multi-instrumentalist. (Center top left) Billy Zoom, guitarist of X. (Center bottom left, seated) Exene Cervenka and John Doe of X, and me. (Center top right) Belinda sitting on the back porch of the shack. (Center bottom right) Jane and me after one too many. (Top right) Margot playing my bass at the same party. (Bottom right) Me on the Rogers drum kit at the shack.

Pages 28–29: (Left and right) Go-Go's get-together at "the shack" in Beverly Glen.

Page 30: (Top) Me and Charlotte. (Bottom) Jane, myself, and Charlotte at the apartment Jane and I shared on Hollywood Boulevard.

Pages 32–33: Me posing in the bathroom at the apartment on Hollywood Boulevard.

Page 34: One of several bathroom shots from the Whisky a Go Go in 1979.

Pages 36–37: Onstage at the Whisky.

Page 39: Babe! Aka Belinda.

Pages 40–41: More bathroom shots at the Whisky.

Pages 42–43: (Left) A 1981 flyer for a gig at the Old Waldorf in San Francisco. (Right) One more photo at the Hollywood Boulevard apartment.

Page 44: Jane and Ginger during our San Francisco trip.

Page 47: Belinda needed a little sleep during our European tour in 1982.

Page 48: Conversation with a bobby during the UK tour with Madness in 1980.

Pages 50–51: (Left) Photo booth pictures with me, Kathy, and Belinda. (Right) Kathy's first show playing with the Go-Go's at the Roxy.

Pages 52–55: Performing at the Whisky.

Page 56: Me and Jane, 1980.

Pages 58–59: (Left) My 1980 calendar marked up with tour dates. Also notice written on the calendar "Robbed New Year's Eve." Jane and I went to see Ultravox at the Whisky. We came home and realized our apartment had been broken into. Happy New Year 1980! (Right) Jane in the back of my pickup truck riding from San Francisco to Los Angeles.

Page 60: (Top left) Joan Jett and me backstage at the Starwood in West Hollywood. (Top right) Jerry Nolan, the drummer for the New York Dolls, and me. (Bottom left) Belinda. (Bottom right) Belinda, Relah, and me.

Page 61: (Top left / Top right) Me and Connie Clark, the Go-Go's hairdresser. (Bottom left) Belinda in Polaroid land. (Bottom right) Jane and Babe.

Pages 62 and 65: Polaroids of the band touring the US in a 12-seater van.

Page 66: Recording *Beauty and the Beat* with our producer Richard Gottehrer and engineer Rob Freeman.

Pages 68–69: (Left) Taking a break during recording. (Right) A flyer advertising our appearance on *SNL*.

Pages 70–71: (Left) Paul Reubens, always the gentleman, sent us a telegram wishing us luck. (Right) Recording *Beauty and the Beat* with my drum tech Anton Fig, who was also the drummer on David Letterman's show.

Page 73: Opening for the Rolling Stones in 1981.

Pages 74–75: (Left) Sting. (Right) Stewart Copeland.

Pages 76–77: (Far left) Andy Summers and his girlfriend and (center) me and Belinda while we were out on tour with the Police. (Right) Andy Summers.

Pages 78–79: (Left) Bette Midler dropped by the recording studio while we were working on *Vacation*. (Right) An all-access badge from the Rolling Stones show.

Pages 80–81: (Left) Meeting Johnny Cash. This was another wow moment. By the way, that's his son John Jr. to the right. (Right) Tammy Wynette of "Stand by Your Man" fame on the left.

Pages 82–83: (Left and right) Touring Middle America. When is the last time you saw Belinda playing pinball in sweats?